Herbert Puchta & Jeff Stranks

G. Gerngross C. Holzmann P. Lewis-Jones

American! MORE! ②

Student's Book

CAMBRIDGE
UNIVERSITY PRESS

HELBLING
LANGUAGES

	Grammar	Language Focus and Vocabulary	Skills	MORE!
UNIT 1 New start	• simple past • simple past endings • disagreeing and correcting	• clubs and activities	• ask about favorite things • talk about clubs and activities • read and understand a web page • listen and complete a table about people • talk about hobbies • read about after school clubs • write about after school clubs	Learn **MORE** through English **A short history of California**
UNIT 2 A great movie!	• simple past irregular verbs	• TV shows and movies	• talk about movies and events • talk about TV • talk about past actions • read a story and find mistakes • write about your weekend **A Song 4 U** *Waiting for you*	**Check your progress** Units 1 and 2 Learn **MORE** about culture **The United States of America** Read **MORE** for pleasure **Storytelling**
UNIT 3 Vacations	• simple past negative, questions, and short answers • question words	• transportation **Sounds right** the /i/sound	• talk about past actions • talk about transportation • talk about vacations • listen and order pictures for a story • read about a jungle trip • write about a trip **A Song 4 U** *Going places*	Learn **MORE** through English **Geographical features of South America**
UNIT 4 Do you know him?	• comparisons	• physical appearance **Sounds right** /æ/	• talk about opinions • describe people • learn about Atlantis • read about animals from Atlantis • write about an animal from Atlantis	**Check your progress** Units 3 and 4 Learn **MORE** about culture **National Parks in the U.S.** Read **MORE** for pleasure **A brave little dog**
UNIT 5 Making plans	• *be going to* • *have to*	• jobs around the house	• talk about future plans • listen to a play and choose answers • read a letter and choose the correct picture • talk about your perfect holiday • write a letter from camp **A Song 4 U** *Hey, let's travel, here we come!*	Learn **MORE** through English **Robots**
UNIT 6 Rules	• *should/shouldn't* • adverbs of manner	• school subjects **Sounds right** a chant	• talk about shapes • talk about school subjects • talk about rules • say how you do things • read about a drama school • listen to a dialogue about borrowing things • ask if you can borrow something • write about things you should and shouldn't do at home	**Check your progress** Units 5 and 6 Learn **MORE** about culture **School life in the U.S.** Read **MORE** for pleasure **The school for magic**

	Grammar	Language Focus and Vocabulary	Skills	MORE!
UNIT 7 On the weekend	• time prepositions: *on, at, in* • present continuous for future	• sports **Sounds right** /tʃ/	• make suggestions • talk about sports • talk about future plans • read about what people do on the weekend • talk about what you do on the weekend • listen and complete diaries about people's plans for the weekend • write about your weekend **A Song 4 U** *Weekend*	**Learn MORE through English** **The feeling of happiness**
UNIT 8 It hurts!	• past continuous • superlatives	• aches and pains	• say what someone was doing • talk about sickness • read about Amazonia and answer questions • listen and complete an animal quiz • read a letter and answer questions • write a letter to a student who is ill	**Check your progress** Units 7 and 8 **Learn MORE about culture** **Sports in the United States** **Read MORE for pleasure** **The world of birds: the biggest and the smallest**
UNIT 9 Guess what?	• past continuous vs. simple past • *one/ones* • quantity *a lot of, much, many*	• emotions	• give reasons • talk about emotions • read a story and match sentences • listen to a story and order pictures • tell and listen to a story • write an ending to a story	**Learn MORE through English** **Famous modern authors for teenagers**
UNIT 10 Shouldn't we ask?	• *should/shouldn't* • conjunctions: *and/ so/but/because*	• directions and places	• use large numbers • give advice • ask for and give directions • listen and read directions • identify buildings • write an email with directions **A Song 4 U** *Looking for Liz*	**Check your progress** Units 9 and 10 **Learn MORE about culture** **The history of the car** **Read MORE for pleasure** **Looking for Keiko**
UNIT 11 It won't rain	• *will/won't* • *might/might not*	• weather	• make excuses • talk about the weather • read about different places and match to the correct photo • listen and draw weather symbols on a map • talk about the weather • talk about your future • write about your future	**Learn MORE through English** **Aurora Borealis—the Northern Lights**
UNIT 12 What if …?	• *If* clauses • possessive pronouns • questions with *Whose?*	• vacations **Sounds right** /i/ /ɪ/	• talk about alternatives • suggestions and preferences • do a quiz about your book • listen and check answers to the quiz • write about your next vacation **A Song 4 U** *We are on vacation*	**Check your progress** Units 11 and 12 **Learn MORE about culture** **Extreme weather** **Read MORE for pleasure** **Strange weather stories**

Wordlist

In this unit

You learn
- simple past
- simple past endings
- disagreeing and correcting
- words for clubs and activities

and then you can
- ask about favorite things
- talk about clubs and activities

① Listen and read.

Sally Hi, Olivia. Are you OK?

Olivia Hi, Sally. Yeah, I'm OK. Well, sort of OK. New York's nice, but I miss California. I arrived last month, and I still don't know anyone here.

Sally Yes, you do! You know me!

Olivia Yes, sorry, you're right. But things were very different in California.

Sally Tell me a little about it.

Olivia Well, we lived in San Diego. Our house was really big, and it was really close to my school. I walked to school in five minutes.

Sally What was the school like?

Olivia It was great. I had a lot of friends there.

Sally What were the teachers like?

Olivia Well, the P.E. teacher wasn't very nice, but the others were great.

Sally What was your favorite subject?

Olivia Drama. I loved it. I was in all the school plays.

Sally Drama? That's my favorite, too! Listen, Olivia, come with me to the drama club here. It's on Tuesdays.

Olivia Tuesdays? Oh no. That's a problem. I joined the school choir yesterday, and it meets on Tuesdays, I think.

Sally No, it doesn't—it meets on Thursdays, from four to five. I know—I'm in choir too!

Olivia That's great! You know, Sally—maybe I don't miss California after all!

2 **Circle T (True) or F (False) for the sentences below.**

1 Olivia doesn't know anyone in New York. T / F
2 Olivia lived in California. T / F
3 Olivia's school was 10 minutes from her house. T / F
4 Olivia liked all the teachers. T / F
5 Sally doesn't like drama. T / F
6 The school choir meets on Tuesdays. T / F

Get talking Asking about favorite things

3 **Listen and repeat.**

A What's your favorite food?   **A** Who's your favorite singer?
B Lasagne.   **B** Shakira.

4 **Work with a partner. Ask and answer questions about the things below. Use the dialogues above.**

place in town

store   movie

month   day of the week   room

color

free-time activity   TV show

movie star   food   *band*

Language Focus

Vocabulary Clubs and activities

  Listen and write the words under the pictures.

> school orchestra   football team   movie club   marching band   chess club
> photography club   drama club   school choir   computer club   art club

Get talking Talking about clubs and activities

  Listen and repeat.

A I want to play chess.
B Join the chess club! It meets
on Tuesdays from five to five thirty.

A I want to play football.
B Join the football team! It meets
on Saturdays from nine to eleven.

3 **Work with a partner. Make similar dialogues. Use the information in the boxes.**

| play chess |
| play football |
| sing |
| use computers |
| watch movies |
| play music |
| take photographs |
| act in plays |

art club: Saturdays, 10:00 a.m.–noon

chess club: Tuesdays, 5:00–5:30 p.m.

drama club: Wednesdays, 1:00–1:45

school choir: Mondays, 1:15–2:00

jazz band: Fridays, 4:30–5:30

photography club: Fridays, 4:00–4:30

computer club: Thursdays, 4:00–5:00

football team: Saturdays, 9:00–11:00

Grammar

Simple past

> Our house **was** really big.   The teachers **were** great.
> I **arrived** last month.   I **walked** to school in five minutes.   We **studied** French.

1 **Complete the rules.**

   i)   There are two simple past forms of the verb "to be": *was* and [1].......

   ii) For the simple past of regular verbs, we add [2]....... to the verb, for example: *play → played*.

   iii) If the verb already ends in –e, just add "d," for example: *like → [3]......*

   iv) If the verb ends in a consonant + –y, change the "y" to "ied," for example: *carry → [4].......*

2 **Complete the sentences with the verbs in the simple past tense.**

want	open	rescue	wait	be (x2)	call	watch

1 There .... two new students in the class yesterday.

2 Pam .... an ice cream.

3 Chris was hot. He .... the window.

4 We .... a great movie at school.

5 The helicopter .... the people on the island.

6 Steve .... me last night about the homework.

7 I .... for 10 minutes.

8 On Monday, I .... late for school.

Simple past endings /t/ /d/ /ɪd/

3a **Write the verbs in the correct columns.**

	/t/	/d/	/ɪd/
waited arrived talked	talked	arrived	waited
wanted jumped tried	....	....	....
called visited watched	....	....	....

3b **Now listen and check your answers.**

4 **Complete the story. Write the verbs in brackets in the simple past tense.**

Yesterday I [1] .... (call) my friend Sandra. I [2] .... (want) some help with my homework. Sandra [3] .... (be) happy to help me, so I [4] .... (walk) over to her house. It [5] .... (be) 9 o'clock at night, and very dark. But I [6] .... (not be) scared. I [7] .... (arrive) at Sandra's house. I knocked on the door and [8] .... (wait). Then I heard a noise in the yard. I [9] .... (try) not to be nervous. "Who's there?" I said. "It's me!" Sandra [10] .... (shout), and she [11] .... (jump) out from behind a bush. I [12] .... (be) really angry at first, but then we [13] .... (laugh) about it. Sandra [14] .... (help) me with my homework, and at 10 o'clock I walked home again.

Grammar Disagreeing and correcting

A They **meet** on Tuesdays.
B No, they don't! They meet on Thursdays.

A He**'s** French.
B No, he isn't! He's Italian.

A I **don't know** anyone here.
B Yes, you do! You know me.

5 **Match the sentences and the answers.**

1 I don't know anyone here.
2 Brazilians speak Spanish.
3 Harry likes pizza.
4 That boy doesn't speak English.
5 She's a nice girl.
6 Olivia isn't from California.
7 Sally was in school last Friday.
8 Olivia wasn't here yesterday.

a) Yes, he does! I talked to him yesterday.
b) Yes, she is! She lived in San Diego.
c) No, she isn't! I don't like her.
d) Yes, you do! You know me.
e) No, she wasn't! She was at home.
f) No, they don't! They speak Portuguese.
g) Yes, she was! I talked to her.
h) No, he doesn't! He hates it.

6 **Listen and check.**

7 **Complete the beginning of each answer.**

1 This pizza isn't very good.   *Yes, it is.* .... It's delicious!
2 We aren't late.   .... We're very late!
3 She doesn't go to our school.   .... She's in my class.
4 They don't live here.   .... They live on my street.
5 The test wasn't difficult.   .... It was very difficult!
6 Sally and Olivia weren't late.   .... They arrived at 9:30.

8 **Write the answers. Use the word in parentheses.**

1 San Diego is the capital of California. (Sacramento)   *No, it isn't. Sacramento's the capital.*
2 Olivia lives in California. (New York)   No, ...
3 Sally and Olivia are sisters. (friends)   No, ...
4 The movie was very good. (really bad)   No, ...
5 Paul and Steve were in school yesterday. (home)   No, ...

9a **Write four sentences that you know are wrong. Write about: *your town / your school / yourself.***

9b **Work with a partner. Say your sentences. Listen to your partner and correct him/her.**

"I'm eighteen."   "No, you're not! You're 15!"
"I like volleyball."   "No, you don't! You hate volleyball!"

Skills

Reading

1 Read Joshua's web page about what American students do in their free time. Then write how many students do these things.

play football   eat ice cream   go dancing   buy magazines

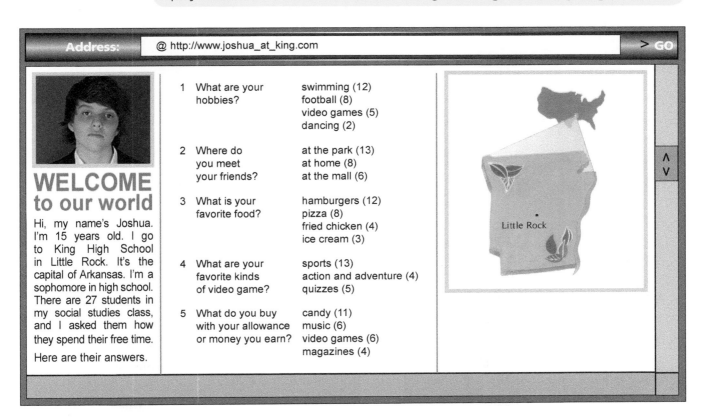

Address: @ http://www.joshua_at_king.com   > GO

WELCOME to our world

Hi, my name's Joshua. I'm 15 years old. I go to King High School in Little Rock. It's the capital of Arkansas. I'm a sophomore in high school. There are 27 students in my social studies class, and I asked them how they spend their free time.

Here are their answers.

1 What are your hobbies?
- swimming (12)
- football (8)
- video games (5)
- dancing (2)

2 Where do you meet your friends?
- at the park (13)
- at home (8)
- at the mall (6)

3 What is your favorite food?
- hamburgers (12)
- pizza (8)
- fried chicken (4)
- ice cream (3)

4 What are your favorite kinds of video game?
- sports (13)
- action and adventure (4)
- quizzes (5)

5 What do you buy with your allowance or money you earn?
- candy (11)
- music (6)
- video games (6)
- magazines (4)

Little Rock

Listening

 2 Listen to Joshua's interview with two of his classmates. Which of the questions from the questionnaire does he **not** ask them?

 3 Listen again. Copy the table into your notebook and complete it with their answers.

		Anna	Paul
1	friends		
2	favorite food		
3	video games		
4	hobbies		

Speaking

4 Work in groups of four. Ask the questions from the survey on page 9 and write down the answers. Report your answers to the class.

> Three of us like swimming, and one of us likes gymnastics.

> All of us watch ......

Reading

5 Read the article. Write the names under the pictures.

Carla   Paul   Ana Marisa

What do you do after school?

We asked you "What do you do after school?" Here are your answers.

At my school there's a cooking club on Tuesdays, and I joined it last month. The teacher is Mr. Bradford—he's great. He shows us how to make a lot of new things. Sometimes I cook with my friend Susana, but usually I cook on my own. I like trying new things. Last week I baked cookies for the first time. They weren't bad! Well, I liked them, and my family liked them, too!
Carla Potter

After school I go home and I make models. I started about a year ago. I need about two weeks to make each model. Then I put it on the shelf in my bedroom. I have about 20 models now. I think I'll need to get another shelf soon. Last year, I tried to start a club for model making at school, but the teachers and other kids weren't interested. Oh well, I have a lot of fun, anyway!
Paul Moore

When I lived in Brazil I joined a horseback riding club. It was great! I learned how to ride horses and take care of them. I love riding! Now I live in the U.S. and there isn't a club in my town, but it isn't a problem. My friend lives on a farm and she has two horses, so twice a week after school (on Wednesdays and Fridays) I go there to ride with her. I think I'm very lucky!
Ana Marisa Azevedo

6 **Who says these things (with different words)?**

1 Sometimes I do my hobby with a friend. ....
2 I do my hobby in my house. ....
3 I learned how to feed and clean a horse. ....
4 I do my hobby two days a week. ....

7 **Circle T (True) or F (False) for the sentences below.**

1 The cooking teacher isn't very good. T / F
2 Carla's family liked the cookies. T / F
3 Paul makes a model every week. T / F
4 Paul started a club at school. T / F
5 Ana Marisa learned to ride in the U.S. T / F
6 Ana Marisa lives on a farm. T / F

Writing for your Portfolio

8 **Write a short text about what you do after school.**

I go to chess club after school on Thursdays. It's great! I started a year ago, and now I am pretty good. I always win when I play. Next year I want to become school chess champion!

A short history of California

Key words

mission	explorers	independent republic
discovered	Native Americans	earthquake
gold	Colonization	population
Union		

  1 Complete the time line. Then listen and check.

California is admitted to the Union.
Spanish explorers arrive in California.

Gold is discovered.
Father Junipero Serra establishes the first mission at San Diego.

10,000 B.C.:	Native Americans are already living in California.
1542:	....
1769:	....
1773:	Colonization begins with the opening of an overland supply route.
1841:	The first wagon train of settlers traveling from the east leaves Missouri for California.
1846:	Settlers at Sonoma proclaim California an independent republic.
1848:	....
1850:	....
1906:	An earthquake and fire destroy much of San Francisco.
2008:	The population of California reaches 36.7 million.

2a **Read the text.**

Women and Calfornia History

California was one of the first states where women won the right to vote in the United States. The California constitution of 1849 gave women the right to own property. In most states, women did not have the right to own property at that time.

In 1911, Californian women won full voting rights, but it would be another nine years before all American women were given full voting rights.

2b **Now answer these questions about your country.**

1 Can women vote in your country?
2 How old should you be to vote?
3 When did men win the right to vote?
4 When did women win the right to vote?

3

Mini-Project Spanish missions in California

Early Spanish settlers established religious outposts in California. These were known as missions. Altogether, 21 missions were established in California. Many cities eventually grew around these missions.

Here are the names of the locations of some of the main missions in California:

San Diego Santa Cruz San Francisco Santa Barbara San Gabriel Lompoc Ventura Fremont Sonoma

i) **Copy the map of California and put the towns/cities listed above in the correct place on it. Use an atlas or the Internet to help you.**

ii) **Find out (use a library or the Internet) which of these cities are named after the original missions.**

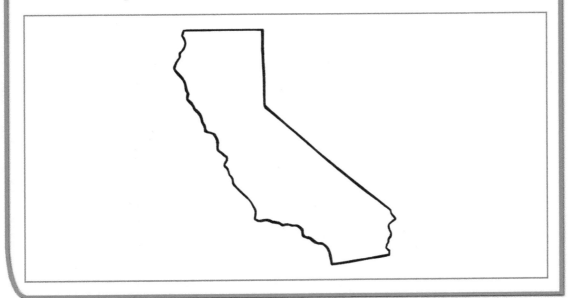

UNIT ② A great movie!

In this unit

You learn
- simple past irregular verbs
- words for TV shows and movies

and then you can
- talk about movies and events
- talk about TV
- talk about past actions

11

1 Listen and read.

Tony I watched a great movie on TV last night.

Sally Really? What was it like?

Tony It was great. It was about some kids who got these weird phone calls. Their cell phone rang, they answered, and then they heard a strange voice. It said, "Your end is near."

Sally Oh, come on! That's an old trick. That's not scary.

Tony That's what the kids thought, too. They believed it was a trick, but each time something really bad happened to them. One boy fell off a building, then a truck hit a girl. They had all kinds of accidents.

Sally Were you scared?

Tony Yes, it was so real. When my cell phone rang at midnight, I got a shock.

Sally What was the name of the movie? Not *The Phone*?

Tony Yes, it was!

Sally That's a terrible movie!

(*Sally's cell phone rings*)

Sally Hang on! Hello?

Voice Your end is near.

Sally Ha, ha, very funny.

Voice Your end is near.

Sally Stop that. Is that you, Fred?

Voice Yes, it is. Listen, Sally. I saw a great movie on TV yesterday.

Sally Oh no. Don't even tell me about it!

2 Match the phrases and form sentences.

1 Tony told Sally about
2 The kids in the movie
3 A voice said, "Your end is near," but the
4 After the phone calls, they
5 Tony liked the movie because
6 Then Sally got a

a got weird phone calls.
b had all kinds of accidents.
c a movie he saw on TV.
d call on her cell phone.
e kids thought it was a trick.
f it was so real.

Get talking Talking about a movie/events

3 Listen and repeat.

A What was the movie like yesterday?
B It was really scary. I loved it.

A What was the movie like yesterday?
B It wasn't very interesting.

4 Work with a partner. Take turns asking each other about movies as Student A. For each answer, Student B should choose two sentences from the box (one from the first column and one from the second column).

A What was the movie like yesterday?

B It was pretty funny. I laughed a lot.

1 It was pretty funny.
2 It wasn't very good.
3 It was terrible.
4 It was OK.
5 It wasn't very exciting.
6 It was excellent.

I hated it.
I really loved it.
I laughed a lot.
Mom and Dad watched it, too.
I don't want the DVD.
I turned it off.

5 Ask and answer about other events in your life.

A What was your weekend / math class like?

B It was awful / great!

Language Focus

Vocabulary TV shows and movies

  1 Listen and write the number of the TV next to the correct description in the list on the left. Check your answers with a partner.

T.V.1 romance movie
.... game show
.... horror movie
.... music video
.... detective movie
.... the news
.... quiz show
.... western
.... sports show
.... science fiction movie
.... nature program
.... cartoon

2 Which TV are they watching? Listen, and then write the number of the correct TV next to each person.

1 David	T.V.1	5 George and Freda	....	9 Jack	....
2 Andrew	....	6 Jane	....	10 Emily and Holly	....
3 Joanna	....	7 Linda and Stephen	....	11 Alexandra	....
4 Veronica	....	8 Paul	....	12 James and Charles	....

Get talking Talking about TV

3 Talk about TV with your partner. Use the sentences to help you.

| I | watch TV for about | one / two / three | hour(s) a day. |

| I | always / usually / sometimes / never | watch TV | in the morning. / in the afternoon. / in the evening. / on the weekend. | I really like (love) / I don't like (hate) | cartoons. / nature programs. / detective shows. / ... |

Grammar

Simple past Irregular verbs

1 **Look at the dialogue on page 14 and complete the table.**
Many verbs in English are irregular. That means we don't add –ed to form the simple past.

verb	ring	hear	say	think	fall	have	see	hit
past form	rang							

Some irregular verbs don't change their form in the simple past, such as *hit, put, and cut*.

hit – hit   *I hit my head on the door.*
cut – cut   *He cut his finger.*
put – put   *We put our coats on.*

2 **Complete the table with the verbs listed on the right.**

go – ¹ went............
have – ²........................
say – ³........................
make – ⁴........................
get – ⁵ got........................
do – ⁶........................
tell – ⁷........................

I ¹ went........... into the living room.
You ²........................ a terrible accident.
"Come to my house," he ³........................ .
She ⁴........................ me a cake.
It ⁵ got........... really cold.
We ⁶........................ our homework after dinner.
"We're American," they ⁷........................ me.

went
got
made
did
told
said
had

3 **Match the simple present verbs to their irregular simple past version.**

| run | leave | take | sit | find | read | come | hold | meet | think |

| came | sat | thought | met | took | ran | read | left | found | held |

4 **Complete the two texts. Use the verbs listed on the right in the simple past tense.**

A The robber ¹........................ into a bank and ²........................
the money. He ³........................ it in a bag and then he
⁴........................ out.

B It ¹.......... a sunny day. Rachel ²................. her bicycle to the park.
She ³.......... on the grass and ⁴.......... her new book.

sit
take
be
go
read
run
put
ride

15 **5** Listen and match the words with the numbers in the picture.

rent ☐ rescue ☐ island ☐ ocean ☐ wave ☐ rocks ☐ gather wood ☐ jump into the ocean ☐

16 **6** Listen to the story and put the pictures in the correct order.

17 **7** Listen again. Put a check next to the verbs you hear. Then write the base form of the verbs.

came ☐ .... was ☐ .... swam ☐ .... took out ☐ .... saw ☐ ....
made ☐ .... began ☐ .... were ☐ .... heard ☐ .... said ☐ ....

Get talking Talking about past actions

8 The chain game. Work in groups of four. Repeat and add one more thing.

A Yesterday, I got up at 7:00 a.m.

B Yesterday, I got up at 7:00 a.m. and had breakfast.

C Yesterday, I got up at 7:00 a.m., had breakfast, and went to school.

D Yesterday, ...

Skills

Reading and listening

1 Read the story and find two mistakes in the picture.

Last Friday evening at 8:00 p.m., the phone rang. It was my best friend, Joseph. He was very excited. "Abigail, come over to my house," he said.

When I arrived at Joseph's place, he took me to the living room. On the red sofa there was a brown bag. "Open it!" he said.

I opened the bag and took out a DVD in its case. "Read it," he said.

I read it: *The Door.*"

"No way," I said. "I don't believe it!"

"Yes," he said. "It's *The Door*!"

The Door is a very famous movie. It is a horror movie. People watch it and terrible things happen.

"A boy from our school watched it," Joseph said. "He had a terrible accident the next day."

"A girl on my street watched it," I said. "Her dog died the next day."

"Let's watch it!" I said.

"I'm not sure," Joseph said. "I'm scared!'

"Don't be silly," I said.

"OK," he said. "Let's watch it!"

Joseph put the DVD into the DVD player. We sat down on the sofa. We were scared. We were very scared. And this is what we saw …

2 Match the sentence halves.

1 Abigail got a phone call from her
2 He invited her to come
3 He showed her
4 It was a movie called
5 *The Door* was a
6 The two friends started

a over to his house.
b *The Door.*
c horror movie.
d friend Joseph.
e to watch it.
f his new DVD.

 3 Listen and find out what Abigail and Joseph saw.

A Song 4 U Waiting for you

4 Complete the song using the words listed on the left. Then listen and check.

were
saw
sat
had (x2)
came
said
made
waited

Last week I ¹............ for you,
But you never ²............ .
Yesterday I telephoned you
It's always the same.

And here I am again,
Sitting by the phone.
Thinking "Where are you?
Why am I alone?"

You ³............ my best friend
You made me laugh when I was sad.
You were my best friend
The best I ever ⁴............ . (x 2)

I ⁵............ you three days ago,
You were in the park.
You ⁶............ and read for hours and hours,
Until it was dark.

You always ⁷............ "hello,"
But now you never do.
Tell me, what went wrong,
Between me and you?

I was your best friend
I ⁸............ you laugh when you were sad.
I was your best friend
The best you ever ⁹............ . (x 4)

Writing for your Portfolio

5 Write about how you spent your weekend.

On Saturday I got up at . . .
I had breakfast and then I . . .
In the afternoon . . .
I went to bed at . . .

On Sunday . . .

Check your progress Units 1 and 2

1 Complete the words.

1 f _ _ _ _ _ _ l t _ _ m
2 c _ _ _ _ _ _ r club
3 c _ _ _ s club
4 p _ _ _ _ _ _ _ _ _ y club
5 school c _ _ _ r
6 school o _ _ _ _ _ _ a   ☐ 6

2 Complete the kinds of movies and TV shows listed below.

1 w _ _ _ _ _ _
2 g _ _ _   s _ _ _
3 h _ _ _ _   m _ _ _ _
4 s _ _ _ _ _ _   f _ _ _ _ _ _   m _ _ _ _
5 c _ _ _ _ _ _
6 q _ _ _   s _ _ _   ☐ 6

3 Complete the dialogue.

A Where ¹ .... you on Sunday afternoon?
B I ² .... at home.
A ³ .... you alone?
B No, I ⁴ .... My brother and sister ⁵ .... with me. We ⁶ .... a good detective show on TV. And then we ⁷ .... games on the computer.   ☐ 7

4 Write the simple past form of the verbs.

1 play ....   4 try ....
2 like ....   5 carry ....
3 study ....   ☐ 5

5 Complete the answers.

1 **A** He's a good football player.
   B No .... ! He's terrible!
2 **A** This movie isn't very interesting.
   B Yes .... ! It's great.

3 **A** It was cold yesterday.
   B No .... ! It was pretty warm.
4 **A** You were late today.
   B No .... ! I arrived at school at eight o'clock.
5 **A** They don't live in a big house.
   B Yes .... ! Their house is really big.
6 **A** She loves cartoons.
   B No .... ! She hates cartoons.   ☐ 12

6 Complete the text. Use the simple past form of the verb in brackets.

Last year my family ¹ .... (go) to Mexico on vacation. We ² .... (meet) a lot of new people and I ³ .... (take) a lot of photographs. We ⁴ .... (stay) in a good hotel near the beach, and there ⁵ .... (be) a lot of things to do there. Unfortunately, on the first day I ⁶ .... (have) an accident. I ⁷ .... (hit) my head on the bathroom door and then I ⁸ .... (cut) my finger, so for two days I ⁹ .... (read) a lot of books and ¹⁰ .... (play) games on my laptop! After that, I ¹¹ .... (do) a lot of different activities—swimming, sailing, and so on. When we ¹² .... (leave), I ¹³ .... (be) really tired! I ¹⁴ .... (tell) Dad that I needed another vacation!   ☐ 14

TOTAL ☐ 50

My progress so far is ...

😊 great!   ☐
😐 good.   ☐
☹️ poor.   ☐

The United States of America

1 **Read the texts below and match them to the correct picture. Then write the name of the state.**

1 Hi. How's it going? My name's Joe. I live in Missouri. The Gateway Arch is in my state. It's 200 meters high. You can get an elevator to the top. It's amazing.

2 Hi, I'm Sarah and I'm from New York City. My favorite landmark is 443.5 meters high. It has 73 elevators and 6,500 windows. There is a fantastic view of the city from the top floor. Can you guess what it is? It's the Empire State Building, of course.

3 Hi, my name's Tanya, and I want to be an astronaut. I'm from Alabama, so I often visit the Space and Rocket Center here. My favorite landmark is the Apollo 11 Launch Vehicle. In 1969, Neil Armstrong, Michael Collins, and Edwin "Buzz" Aldrin traveled to the moon in Apollo 11.

4 Hi, my name's Mark. I'm a big football fan from California. My favorite landmark is the Pasadena Rose Bowl. Every year, they hold college football games here.

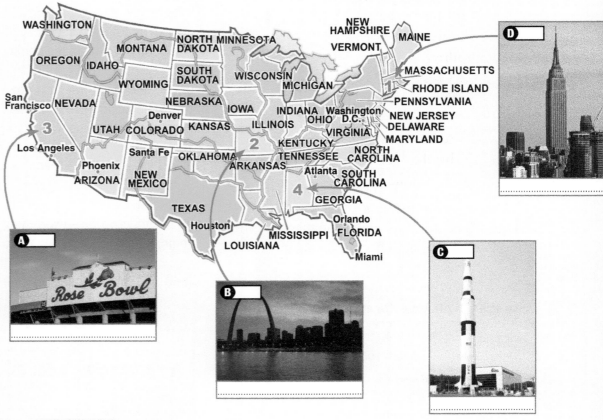

2 **Over 2 U!** **Draw a map of your country. Include:**

1 a historic landmark
2 a modern landmark
3 a famous sports stadium
4 a famous bridge or tower

Write a short paragraph about one of the landmarks.

MORE! Now you can watch Episode 1 of *Kids in NYC!*

Learn MORE about Culture

It was Friday afternoon. Everyone was tired. "OK," Miss Cross said. "Close your books. Who wants to tell an interesting story?"

Five or six hands went up in the air.

"Let's start with Sara," said Miss Cross.

"My family—that's me, my mom, my dad and my twelve-year-old brother, Michael—went to Arizona in July," she said. "We went to the Grand Canyon. It was really beautiful and we had a great time exploring the area."

"Boring!" said Andrew Wilson.

"Shhh!" said Miss Cross. Sara went on. "One day, my brother and I were climbing some rocks."

"So what?" said Andrew Wilson.

"Well, I saved my brother's life."

"I don't believe you," shouted Kevin Biggins.

"Quiet! Let Sara tell her story," Miss Cross said.

"My brother followed me up some rocks near our campground. I was above him when I heard a sound like a rattle. I immediately thought it was a rattlesnake."

"A what?" said Andrew Wilson.

"A rattlesnake. I know a lot about rattlesnakes. I could see the snake, though my brother could not. It was a western diamondback rattlesnake. It could kill him with one bite. I told my brother to calmly move back down off the rocks," said Sara.

"We don't believe you," said some of the students.

"There are no rattlesnakes in the Grand Canyon," said Andrew Wilson.

"There's one way to find out," said Miss Cross. "Let's check on the Internet!"

This is what the students found on the Internet:

Rattlesnakes live in North and South America. There are 36 species of rattlesnakes. In Arizona, there are 13 species. Rattlesnakes make venom to kill their prey. About one percent of rattlesnake bites in Arizona result in human deaths.

The western diamondback rattlesnake can grow to more than 150 centimeters long. It is the largest rattlesnake in the western part of the United States. It bites, and kills, more humans than any other rattlesnake species. Some western diamondback rattlesnakes live in the Grand Canyon.

For **MORE!** Go to www.cambridge.org/elt/americanmore and take a quiz on this text.

In this unit

You learn
- simple past negative, questions, and short answers
- question words
- words for transportation

and then you can
- talk about past actions
- talk about transportation
- talk about vacations

20 **1** **Listen and read.**

Lisa Hi, Harry. I didn't see you at our study club yesterday. Where were you?

Harry I went to Lake Michigan with my parents and sister.

Lisa How cool! Did you like it? How did you get there? Did you take an airplane? How long did it take?

Harry It was really great. We didn't fly. We drove there with some family friends. It only took about four hours.

Lisa What did you do at the lake?

Harry We went swimming. We also went water-skiing.

Lisa Did you go fishing?

Harry No, we didn't. We didn't have enough time.

Lisa How long did you stay?

Harry Three days. The only bad thing was that I lost my wallet.

Lisa Oh no! Did you have a lot of money in it?

Harry No, I didn't—only $5.00, but the photo Sally took of us at her birthday party last year was in it.

Lisa That's too bad!

2 **Match the questions and answers.**

1 How did Harry and his family travel to the lake?
2 How long did they stay?
3 Did he like it?
4 What did they do at the lake?
5 Did they go fishing?
6 What bad thing happened to Harry?

a No, they didn't.
b Yes, he did.
c They traveled by car.
d They stayed for three days.
e He lost his wallet.
f They went swimming and water-skiing.

Get talking Talking about past actions

 3 **Listen and repeat.**

A What did Sandra do in New York City?
B She went to a museum.

A What did Sandra do in Florida?
B She visited a water park.

4 **Work with a partner. Ask and answer about Sandra.**

A What did Sandra do in…
B She…

Arizona—fly over the Grand Canyon

Washington, D.C.—visit the Washington Monument

St. Louis—ride to the top of the Gateway Arch

New York—go to Niagara Falls

Texas—see the Alamo

Tennessee—take photos

Language Focus

Vocabulary Transportation

22 **1** Write the numbers next to the correct word on the left. Then listen and check.

- ☐ bike
- ☐ metro
- ☐ school bus
- ☐ car
- ☐ bus
- ☐ train
- ☐ trolleybus
- ☐ plane
- ☐ taxi
- ☐ moped
- ☐ ferryboat
- ☐ motorcycle

Sounds right The /i/ sound

23 **2** Listen and repeat the words. In which words do you hear an /i/ sound?

1 bike   2 metro   3 taxi   4 plane   5 ferryboat   6 have   7 come   8 arrive

Get talking Talking about transportation

24 **3** Read the dialogue. Fill in the blank. Then listen and repeat.

Assistant	Hello. Can I help you?
Customer	Hi. How much is a ticket to Pittsburgh?
Assistant	One-way or round trip?
Customer	Round trip, please.
Assistant	Let me see. That's $42.00.
Customer	And what time's the next train?
Assistant	The next train leaves at half past three.
Customer	OK, I'd like two round-trip tickets to Pittsburgh, please.
Assistant	That's $....................... .
Customer	Here you go.
Assistant	Here are your tickets and change. Have a nice trip.
Customer	Thanks.

Grammar

Simple past Negative

1 Look at the dialogue on page 24 and complete the examples and the rule.

1 I .... you at our study club yesterday.
2 We .... fly.
3 We .... enough time.

To talk about the simple past in the negative we add [4]........... (*did not*) in front of the verb. This is the same for all subjects (*I/you/he/she* etc.). It is also the same for regular and irregular verbs.

2 Make the sentences negative.

1 My friends came to my party.   *My friends didn't come to my party.*..............................
2 I saw a great movie yesterday.   ....
3 They called me from New York.   ....
4 We told a lot of jokes.   ....
5 You bought a nice pair of jeans.   ....

3 Complete the sentences. Use the affirmative or negative form of the simple past.

1 I ...*didn't write*... to you because I ....*was*........... ill. (not write / be)
2 I .... at 6:00 a.m. because my alarm clock .... (not wake up / not ring)
3 She .... to James because she .... him. (not talk / not see)
4 The shuttle bus .... on time, so we .... our plane. (not arrive / miss)
5 My old camera .... , so I .... a new one. (not work / want)

Simple past Questions and short answers

4 Look at the dialogue on page 24 and complete the questions.

Yes/No questions	Affirmative	Negative
1 .... an airplane?	Yes, I **did**.	No, I **didn't**.
2 .... fishing?	Yes, we **did**.	No, we **didn't**.
3 .... a lot of money in it?	Yes, I **did**.	No, I **didn't**.

5 Complete the questions and the short answers.

1 **A** *Did they arrive*.. after midnight? (arrive)   **B** Yes, *they did*...... .
2 **A** .... you (pl) .... your trip? (enjoy)   **B** No, ...
3 **A** .... your parents .... with you? (come)   **B** No, ...
4 **A** .... the trip .... a lot of money? (cost)   **B** Yes, ...
5 **A** .... you .... on a trip to the lake? (go)   **B** Yes, ...

Simple past Question words

6 **Look at the dialogue on page 24 and complete the questions.**

Wh- questions	
How long ¹.......... it ....?	(It took) three hours.
What did you ².......... at the ....?	We went swimming.
How long ³.......... you ....?	(We stayed) three days.

7 **Reorder the words to make questions.**

1 you / what / do / did _What did you do_......?
2 you / did / go / when ....?
3 there / get / how / you / did ....?
4 stay / you / did / how long ....?
5 leave / you / did / why ....?

Get talking Talking about vacations

25 **8** **Complete the dialogue with the sentences. Listen and check. Then act it out.**

How long did you stay
  there?
Did you buy a lot?
Hi Lisa. Did you go to
  New York last month?
Did you enjoy it?
What did you like most?

Marcus ¹...

Lisa   Yes, I did.

Marcus ²...

Lisa   Yes, I did. It was fantastic.

Marcus ³...

Lisa   Only for a week.

Marcus ⁴...

Lisa   The stores on Fifth Avenue.

Marcus ⁵...

Lisa   No, I didn't. Just a few souvenirs!

Sounds right

9 **A chant. Listen and repeat.**

26 A **I** didn't do it.
      B You **didn't**? You **didn't**?
      A I **didn't**.
      B Who **did**?
      A The neighbor's bad **kid**.

10 **Ask four people in the class about their vacation. Use the questions below.**

Where did you go on vacation last year?

I went to | Cancun.
Chicago.
Toronto.
San Francisco.

Did you like it?
Did you see...?
What did you see?
How long did you
  stay?
Did your ... go
  with you?
Did you go to a lot
  of museums?
What did you
  like most?

Yes, ... / No, ...
We saw...
Yes, ... / No, ...
Yes, ... / No, ...
I think the...
For... days (weeks).
Yes, ... did. / No, ...
didn't.

Skills

Listening

27 **1** Listen to the story *Khalid's Journey* and put the pictures in the correct order.

2 Work with a partner and write the correct questions for the answers below. Use the question words.

1 Khalid lived in Egypt.
2 There were four trees in his yard.
3 He went to Cairo.
4 Because he didn't have any money for a hotel.
5 He slept there for three days.
6 He told a man about his dream.
7 The man described his dream about a garden with four trees.
8 Khalid went home.
9 He dug a hole under the orange tree.
10 He found a bag of gold!

What...
Why...
Where...
How many...
Who...
How long...

3 Now close your books and use your questions to ask and answer about the story.

Reading and speaking

4 **Read about Mark's trip to the jungle and circle the photos that show how he traveled.**

Hi, I'm Mark. Read about my cool trip into the jungle that I took last year.

JUNGLE TRIP!

Last year, I went to Guatemala with my mom and dad. Guatemala is a country in Central America. We flew there from Mexico. The plane was old and very small. I was a little scared. We rented a jeep at the airport and drove to the old Mayan city of Tikal. Tikal is in the jungle.

During the day, we walked around the old city. Then in the early evening, we climbed to the top of the highest pyramid and watched the sunset. We could hear all the animals in the jungle. They made a lot of noise, especially the monkeys. It was my first trip to the jungle, so I was very excited.

That night, we slept in a tent. I imagined there were jaguars, monkeys, and snakes outside, so I didn't sleep very well. When I woke up, I saw a huge spider at the top of the tent. That was the worst part of the trip!

5 **Work with a partner. Use the words below and ask and answer questions about Mark's trip.**

1 Where / go last year?
2 Who / to Guatemala with?
3 What / do during the day?

4 What noises / hear?
5 Where / stay?
6 What / see in the morning?

A Song 4 U *Going places*

 28 **6** **Listen and complete the song with the words on the left. Then sing along!**

am
was (x 4)
went (x 7)
heard (x 2)
did (x 2)
didn't
are (x 2)
isn't

At first I ¹.............. to Denver.
I ².............. that it was great.
At first I ³.............. to Denver.
My plane ⁴.............. really late.
My room ⁵.............. very small,
three meters wall-to-wall.

Chorus
Why ⁶.............. you go away?
Why ⁷.............. you not just
stay home?

Then I ⁸.............. to Boston.
I ⁹.............. that it was cool.
Then I ¹⁰.............. to Boston.
Oh, I ¹¹.............. such a fool.
I ¹².............. like the food,
the weather ¹³.............. not good.

Chorus (x 2)

Then I ¹⁴.............. to Florida,
it's nice there, people said.
Then I ¹⁵.............. to Florida,
I ¹⁶.............. there—and I fled.
Tourists everywhere.
What ¹⁷.............. they doing there?

Chorus (x 3)

And now I'm home again,
But I ¹⁸.............. all alone
I'm home, but no one's calling me,
I'm sitting by the phone!

My room's so small,
my friends ¹⁹.............. gone,
the weather ²⁰.............. good.

I'd really like to get away
I'd love to take a vacation!! (x 3)

Writing for your Portfolio

7 **Write a short paragraph about a trip you took. Start like this:**

In..., I went to... with my.... We stayed for...

Geographical features of South America

Key words

field	tribe	deep	volcano	waterfall
wool	rain forest	wide	desert	lake

29

1 Take this quiz about South America by placing a check next to the correct answer. Then listen and check.

1 How many people live in South America?
   a) about 400 million ☐   b) about 200 million ☐
   c) about 100 million ☐   d) about 50 million ☐

2 What are the two main languages in South America?
   a) Spanish and French ☐   b) Spanish and Portuguese ☐
   c) French and Portuguese ☐   d) English and Spanish ☐

3 Which is the biggest country in South America?
   a) Venezuela ☐   b) Ecuador ☐   c) Chile ☐   d) Brazil ☐

4 Which four countries are not in South America?
   a) Argentina ☐   b) Bolivia ☐   c) Chile ☐   d) Sweden ☐   e) Brazil ☐
   f) Vietnam ☐   g) Peru ☐   h) Uruguay ☐   i) Iran ☐   j) Colombia ☐
   k) Canada ☐   l) Venezuela ☐

2 Read the texts and match the geographical features with the letters on the map.

1 River ☐
The Amazon is more than 6,400 kilometers long. It flows through many different

countries, including Peru, Colombia, Ecuador, and Brazil. There is more water in this river than any other river in the world.

2 Lake ☐

Lake Titicaca is on the border between Bolivia and Peru. It is 3,810 meters above sea level. It is also a deep lake, in places it is about 180 meters deep. This lake is practically a small ocean. It is more than 190 kilometers long and about 80 kilometers wide. There are also 41 islands in the lake.

3 Waterfall ☐

The Angel Falls in Venezuela are almost 1,000 meters high. In very hot weather the water can evaporate before it reaches the bottom.

4 Desert ☐

The Atacama Desert in Chile is about 1,000 kilometers long. It is also 15 million years old. It is very dry. On average, one millimeter of rain falls here per year.

5 Rain forest ☐

Amazonia is a rain forest that covers over 4 million square kilometers in the countries Brazil, Venezuela, Colombia, Ecuador, and Peru. It produces about 20 percent of Earth's oxygen. More than half of the world's species of plants, insects, and animals live in Amazonia.

3 Read the text and then complete the fact file about Brazil.

FACT FILE

Brazil is the largest country in South America. Its capital city is Brasilia. About 182.8 million people live in Brazil, and the official language is Portuguese. Some important exports from Brazil are oranges and coffee. The important geographical features of Brazil are the Amazon River and Amazonia. One major problem in Brazil is the destruction of the rain forest. Many animals and plants are disappearing as a result. Many peoples that once lived in the rain forest don't exist any more.

Name: _Brazil_

Capital: ....

Population: ....

Official language: ....

Exports: ....

Major geographical features: _Amazon River,_

Problems: _destruction of the rain forest,_

Mini-Project A country in South America

4 **Make a poster about a country in South America. On the poster:**

- put a map with the capital city and one or two additional cities
- put pictures of any important mountains / rivers / lakes / etc.
- put pictures of any animals that are found in the country
- write some sentences using the information you found

Use books or the Internet to find the information.

(If you live in South America, choose a country that is not your country!)

5 **Write a fact file about the country. Use the Internet or a library to help you.**

In this unit

You learn
- comparisons
- words for physical appearance

and then you can
- talk about opinions
- describe people

30

1 **Listen and read.**

Olivia I met a really nice boy at school today. He's got brown hair. Oh, and brown eyes—they're as brown as yours!

Sally Oh, I think I know who you're talking about. That's Harry, my brother!

Olivia Hmm. I think he's cool—cooler than the boys in my class in California.

Sally Really? He's boring! Well, he isn't as interesting as me! I like Ryan. I like boys who have light, curly hair. And he's cuter than Harry! I think he's more interesting, too.

Olivia Sally, did you hear that noise?

Sally Yes, I did. I think it was Harry on the other phone! I'm so mad at him! I'll call you back. Harry, I want to talk to you.

Harry What's the matter?

Sally I don't think it's nice to listen to private conversations.

Harry Sally, I don't know what you're talking about!

Sally My phone conversation with Olivia—you listened to it!

Harry No I didn't!

Mom Sally, don't shout at Harry. It wasn't him—it was me. I wanted to use the phone, but I heard you and Olivia, so I hung it up again. I'm sorry.

Sally Oh. Sorry, Mom.

Mom Don't say sorry to me. Say it to your brother. That's more important.

Sally OK. Sorry, Harry.

Harry Excuse me?

Sally Oh, come on, Harry: I'm really, really, really sorry!

Harry That's better!

2 **Circle T (True) or F (False) for the sentences below.**

1 Harry has brown hair. T / F
2 Olivia prefers the boys in California to Harry. T / F
3 Sally likes boys with blonde hair. T / F
4 Sally thinks Ryan is interesting. T / F
5 Mom wanted to listen to Olivia and Sally on the phone. T / F
6 Harry prefers Sally's second "sorry." T / F

Get talking Opinions

3 **Listen and repeat.**

A Do you like hip-hop?
B Yes, but I think rock music is better.

A I don't think English is very interesting.
B Really? I prefer English to math.

A I love Chinese food.
B Well, I prefer Italian food.

A Do you prefer long or short hair?
B I like them both.

4 **Work with a partner. Ask and answer questions about the things listed below. Use the words in the box to help you.**

Do you like Japanese food?

I prefer Chinese food.

blue eyes / green eyes   swimming / volleyball   Japanese food / pizza
Fridays / Mondays   cats / dogs

I think / don't think X is …	I prefer X.
I like / love X.	I prefer X to Y.
Do you like X?	I like X but I think Y's better.
Do you prefer X or Y?	I don't mind.

Language Focus

Vocabulary Physical appearance

32 **1** **Look at the pictures. Match the numbers to the correct word. Then listen and check.**

Hair color
- [ ] red
- [ ] brown
- [ ] blonde
- [ ] black

Hair type
- [ ] long
- [ ] short
- [ ] straight
- [ ] curly

wavy

Eye color
- [ ] blue - [ ] brown
- [ ] green - [ ] black

- [ ] old
- [ ] young
- [ ] slim
- [ ] big
- [ ] tall
- [ ] short

Get talking Describing people

2 **Read and write the names of the boys under the pictures.**

Kevin is pretty slim. He wears glasses and he has blue eyes. His hair is brown and curly.

Tom wears glasses and he has green eyes and bushy eyebrows. His hair is long, brown, and wavy.

Paul is tall and slim. He doesn't wear glasses. He has brown eyes, and his hair is brown and curly.

Ben is short. He has brown eyes and his hair is long, black, and straight.

1 .... 2 .... 3 .... 4 ....

3 **Work in pairs. Describe a person in your class. Your partner guesses who it is.**

Grammar

Comparisons (1)

1 **Look at the dialogue on page 34 and complete the examples.**

1 I think he's cool—................. than the boys in my class in California.
2 And he's cuter than Harry! I think he's ...., too

a To compare two things, we use **adjective + er [+ than]**
  (old) She's **older than** me.
  (cool) He's **cooler than** the boys in my class
     in California.
  (hot) Today is **hotter than** yesterday.
b Be careful with spelling! curly → cur**lier**   hot → hot**ter**
c The words *good* and *bad* are irregular:
  (good) His English is **better than** mine.
  (bad) The weather today is **worse than** yesterday.

She's faster than me.

Comparisons (2)

2 **Write the comparative forms of these adjectives.**

1 strong   *stronger than*
2 tall   ....
3 young   ....
4 funny   ....
5 cold   ....
6 short   ....
7 slim   ....
8 good   ....
9 long   ....
10 wavy   ....
11 straight ....
12 bad   ....

With adjectives that are longer (two syllables or more) we use **more + adjective [+ than]**
That's **more important**.
He's **more interesting than** Fred.

4 **Write answers to the questions. Begin each answer with "Yes."**

1 Are Ferraris expensive? (Porsches)
  Yes, they're more expensive than Porsches.
2 Is it hot this year? (last year) ....
  ....
3 Is the test difficult? (last week's) ....
  ....
4 Is Canada big? (the U.S.) ....
  ....
5 Is basketball exciting? (volleyball) ....
  ....
  ....

3 **Use the adjectives in parentheses to write comparisons.**

1 James / Mike (tall) *James is taller than*
  Mike.
2 Her hair / my hair (long) ....
  ....
3 February / December (short) ....
  ....
4 Paula / Monica (funny) ....
  ....
5 Pizza / spaghetti (good) ....
  ....

Comparisons (3)

5 **Look at the dialogue on page 34 and complete the examples.**

They're ¹................ brown .... yours.
He isn't ²................ interesting .... me!

We can also compare two things like this:
... **(not) as [adjective] as** ....

He's **as tall as** his father.   Fred is**n't as tall as** Sue.

6 **Compare the pictures. Write sentences. Use *not as ... as*.**

1   Steve / Jim (strong)
....

2   The Grand Hotel / The Palace Hotel (good)
....

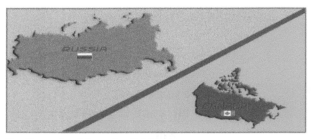

3   Canada / Russia (big)
....

4   New England / Mexico (hot)
....

7 **Use the words to make *(not) as... as* comparisons.**

1   I / not tall / my sister
    I'm not as tall as my sister.

2   Mike / not short / Jack
    ....

3   His hair / not long / his sister's
    ....

4   Sue / not old / her brother
    ....

5   Your mother / not old / my grandmother
    ....

6   Jeff / not good-looking / Tom
    ....

Sounds right /æ/

8 **A chant. Listen and repeat.**

33   S**a**m the r**a**t h**a**d a ch**a**t
         with Billy the b**a**t and Carl the c**a**t
         as they s**a**t on a m**a**t.

Skills

Reading and listening

 1 **Read this extract from a newspaper. Then listen and put a check next to what the teenagers say about Atlantis.**

Researchers discover sunken city of
Atlantis

American researchers say they believe that the sunken city of Atlantis lies 1.5 kilometers below sea level, 80 kilometers off the coast of Cyprus.

The Greek philosopher Plato was the first person to write about Atlantis. He said, "Atlantis was larger than North Africa and Asia together."

Jonathan

- ☐ I believe Atlantis existed.
- ☐ I think it was closer to Japan than Europe.
- ☐ I think Atlantis is older than Europe.

Dan

- ☐ I am sure Atlantis existed.
- ☐ In 2222, Atlantis will come back out of the waves of the ocean.
- ☐ When this happens, many animals in the world will die.

Rachel

- ☐ Atlantis never existed.
- ☐ Atlantis was not home to strange creatures.
- ☐ The story of Atlantis is science fiction.

Naomi

- ☐ I don't think Atlantis existed.
- ☐ I believe Atlantis is larger than the U.S.
- ☐ I believe stories of underwater temples, mysterious palaces, etc., are just fairy tales.

Speaking and reading

2 **Say what you think about Atlantis.**

I	believe / don't believe	that	Atlantis existed. lots of temples, houses, streets, and people sank in the ocean. Atlantis was where the Caribbean is today. strange animals lived in Atlantis.

3 Here are the cards for animals that the students in Exercise 1 imagined lived in Atlantis. Read the cards and then circle T (True) or F (False) below.

THE RUCKLE
The Ruckle was very exotic. It was half-animal and half-bird, but it didn't fly. It was as big as a rabbit. It was friendly, and many people had ruckles in their homes as pets.

THE BUGBOY
The Bugboy was a small reptile. It was as small as a mouse, but as dangerous as a snake. In fact, it was as poisonous as a rattlesnake. Every year, hundreds of people died from its bite.

THE SNAPKLE
The Snapkle was a kind of dragon. It lived in the mountains outside Atlantis. It was as big as an elephant, but it wasn't as nice as an elephant. In fact, it was very ugly.

THE HIPCOP
The Hipcop wasn't as friendly as the Ruckle, but it was also a popular pet. It was as smart as a chimpanzee.

1 People kept Ruckles in their homes. T / F
2 The Hipcop was friendlier than the Ruckle. T / F
3 The Snapkle was bigger than an elephant. T / F
4 The Bugboy was a kind of rattlesnake. T / F
5 The Hipcop wasn't as smart as a chimpanzee. T / F
6 The Bugboy wasn't very dangerous. T / F

4 Draw your own animal from Atlantis and give it a name.

Writing for your Portfolio

5 Write a gaming card for your animal from Atlantis.

MORE fun with Fido

I'm hungrier than a wolf.

I'm smarter than an owl.

I'm fatter than an elephant.

KEEP OUT!

Check your progress Units 3 and 4

1 **Write the names of the type of transportation.**

1 .... 2 ....

3 .... 4 ....

5 .... 6 .... ☐ **6**

2 **Complete the words.**

1 hair – c _ _ _ _   4 hair color – bl _ _ _
2 eyes – gr _ _ _   5 hair – st_ _ _ _ _ _
3 physical – sl _ _   6 age – y _ _ _ _ ☐ **6**

3 **Complete the dialogues.**

A What ¹........................ you do at the lake yesterday?
B I ²........................ swimming and ³........................ a lot of pictures of the beautiful scenery!
A ⁴........................ you go on a boat trip?
B Yes, I ⁵........................ . It ⁶........................ great!

A Which group do you think is ⁷........................ (good)? U2 or The Rolling Stones?
B U2 definitely. Their music is ⁸........................ (interesting) than The Rolling Stones'.
A I think U2's music is boring! ☐ **8**

4 **Write questions.**

1 ....?
We went sightseeing.
2 ....?
We went by train.

3 ....?
We went to Florida.
4 ....?
It took five hours.
5 ....?
We got back yesterday. ☐ **10**

5 **Complete the dialogue with the correct verb or comparative form.**

A ¹........................ (you / go) to Mexico on vacation last year?
B Yes, I ²........................
A ³........................ (you / enjoy) it?
B Yes, the weather was ⁴........................ (good) than in Florida, where we went last year. It was ⁵........................ (hot).
A Was it ⁶........................ (expensive) than Florida?
B No, I think it was ⁷........................ (cheap).
A How long ⁸........................ (you / stay) there?
B Two weeks.
A ⁹........................ (you / swim) a lot?
B Yes, we ¹⁰........................ . Every day! ☐ **10**

6 **Write five sentences to describe your best friend.**

....
....
....
....
....

☐ **10**

TOTAL ☐ **50**

My progress so far is ...

☺ great! ☐

😐 good. ☐

☹ poor. ☐

National Parks in the U.S.

35

1 Listen to Emma talk about her visit to Redwood National Park. Complete the information to the right about the trees.

REDWOOD NATIONAL PARK

Redwood trees

Height:	
Number of years to grow:	
Age:	

2 Read about the Colorado Rockies and Yellowstone National Park. Then answer the questions.

1 Who lived in the Rocky Mountains?
2 Why are the Rockies called "the roof of America"?
3 How high are the tallest mountains in the Rockies?
4 What is Yellowstone famous for?
5 How often does Yellowstone erupt?

Do you know?

The first national park in the U.S. was Yellowstone National Park. It opened in 1872 and was the first national park in the world.

THE COLORADO ROCKIES

The Rocky Mountains were home to the Apache, Blackfoot, and Sioux Indians. The Rockies stretch from Alaska all the way to New Mexico. The Rockies are high! The Colorado Rockies are the tallest. People call them "the roof of America" because the tops of the mountains here are 4,401 meters high. The Colorado Rockies are popular for mountain climbing, fishing, hunting, and skiing.

YELLOWSTONE NATIONAL PARK

This park is in Wyoming and is older than any other national park. It is famous for hot springs and grizzly bears. Some of the bears are huge. They can weigh as much as 700 kilograms. There are also wolves and bison living in the park.

The park is 8,980 square kilometers. Before human history, a huge volcanic eruption covered the area with ash. Yellowstone usually erupts every 600,000 years. The last eruption was 640,000 years ago!

3 **Over 2 U!** Choose a mountain range and a national park in your country and write a description of them. Then tell your partner.

MORE! Now you can watch Episode 2 of *Kids in NYC!* DVD

A brave little dog

August 5, 2004, was a very hot day in Springfield. Judith Crowe and her six-year-old son, Jeff, wanted to go swimming in the river near their home. They got in the car with their pet dog, Spot, and drove to the river. When they got there, Judith, Jeff, and Spot went for a swim in the water. Spot was a very good swimmer. In fact, he was better than Jeff.

Judith and her son played and swam in the water for a long time. All the time, Spot was with them. After about an hour, Judith got thirsty. "Stay here for a minute, Jeff," she said, and she got out of the water. She walked back to her car to get some water to drink.

When she turned around, she got a shock. Jeff was in the middle of the river. The water was deeper and more dangerous there. He was in trouble.

Jeff's mother jumped into the water and

started to swim. But Spot was faster than Judith, and he got to the boy first.

The boy put his arms around the dog. But he was bigger than the dog and he was heavier, too. The boy and the dog both disappeared under the water.

Jeff's mother didn't know what to do. Then suddenly, she saw the dog again. Jeff was on Spot's back. Spot swam to the side of the river. Jeff and Spot got out of the water. Judith's son was safe. She was a very happy mother!

For MORE! Go to www.cambridge.org/elt/americanmore and take a quiz on this text.

In this unit

You learn
- *be going to*
- *have to*
- words for jobs around the house

and then you can
- talk about future plans

36 **1** **Listen and read.**

Mrs. Elton	Hey everyone! I have an email from Aunt Maria. She arrives tomorrow.
Mr. Elton	My favorite sister-in-law. Is she going to sleep in my office?
Mrs. Elton	Yes, so you have to put all your books and papers away … and Harry, this living room's a mess. You have to put all the DVDs back on the shelves.
Harry	But I'm still watching them.
Mr. Elton	Harry, don't argue.
Mrs. Elton	… and then you have to clean your room.
Harry	But Aunt Maria isn't going to stay in my room, so why do I have to clean it? Sally doesn't have to clean her room!
Sally	My room is already clean!
Harry	Little Miss Perfect!
Mrs. Elton	Stop it, you two. Harry, you're going to do what I ask, and Sally, you're going to help me with cleaning the rest of the house.
Harry	What about Dad?
Mrs. Elton	He's going to take out the garbage, and then he has to clean his office. OK? Let's get going!

2 **Put a check by the correct answer.**

1 Aunt Maria arrives
- ☐ tomorrow.
- ☐ in two days.
- ☐ next week.

2 Who has to put all books and papers away?
- ☐ Sally
- ☐ Dad
- ☐ Harry

3 Harry has to put the DVDs back
- ☐ in Sally's room.
- ☐ on the shelves in the living room.
- ☐ on the shelves in his bedroom.

4 Dad is going to
- ☐ help with the dusting.
- ☐ clean the windows.
- ☐ take out the garbage.

Get talking Talking about future plans

3 **Match the words with the pictures.**

a go skateboarding
b visit my aunt and uncle

c do my homework
d see my friends

e buy some music
f watch DVDs

37

4 **Listen and repeat.**

A What are you going to do this weekend?
B I'm going to visit my aunt and uncle.

A What are you going to do this weekend?
B I'm going to see my friends.

5 **Work with a partner. Ask and answer questions about what you are doing this weekend.**

Language Focus

Vocabulary Jobs around the house

1 **Look at the picture and complete the sentences with the correct names.**

1 .....Peter..... is cleaning his room.
2 .... is taking out the garbage.
3 .... is washing the dishes.
4 .... is doing the shopping.
5 .... is doing the vacuuming.

6 .... is doing the dusting.
7 .... is cooking dinner.
8 .... is ironing the clothes.
9 .... is making her bed.

2 **Listen and write the correct number of ✓ and ✗ in the boxes below.**

love ✓✓✓✓
sort of like ✓✓✓
don't mind ✓✓
hate ✗

3 **Talk about the jobs you like/hate doing at home.**

I hate washing the dishes.

I don't mind making my bed.

Grammar

Be going to

① **Put the example sentences in order, and then check against the dialogue on page 44.**

going / he's / garbage / the / out / to / take
going / room / isn't / Aunt / in / to / stay / my / Maria
Is / she / to / sleep / my / office / in / going

Affirmative			Negative		
I'm		clean the house.	I'm not		clean the house.
He/she/it's	**going to**	buy a new camera.	He/she/it **isn't**	**going to**	buy a new camera.
You/we/they**'re**		make dinner.	You/we/they **aren't**		make dinner.

Questions	Short answers	
	Affirmative	**Negative**
Am I going to be late?	Yes, you **are**.	No, you **aren't**.
Are you going to be late?	Yes, I **am**.	No, I'm **not**.
Is he/she/it going to be late?	Yes, he/she/it **is**.	No, he/she/it **isn't**.
Are we/you/they going to be late?	Yes, we/you/they **are**.	No, we/you/they **aren't**.

② **Write what these people are (not) going to do in the future.**

1   Mark: buy a sports car (yes) ....
....
....

2   Tony and Liz: go on a trip around the
world (yes) ....
....
....

3   I: learn to fly a plane (no) ....
....
....

4   Harry: move to another country (no) ....
....
....

5   Linda: have a big 18th birthday party (yes)
....
....

③ **Write questions. Then work with a partner and ask and answer.**

1   you / see friends / weekend
Are you going to see friends on the
weekend ....?

2   your family / go / on vacation / this year
....
....?

3   your father / come / to school tomorrow
....
....?

4   you / stay home tomorrow
....
....?

4 Talk about these people's plans with your partner. Use the words below.

A Picture 1. What's she going to do?

B She's going to do her homework.

go grocery shopping   stay at a friend's house
do her homework   play volleyball

have to

5 **Look at the dialogue on page 44 and complete the examples.**

1 You .... put all your books and papers away.
2 You .... clean your room.
3 Sally .... to clean her room.

Affirmative		
I/You/We/You/They	**have to**	put all the DVDs on the shelves.
He/She/It	**has to**	work.

Negative		
I/You/We/You/They	**don't have to**	put all the DVDs on the shelves.
He/She/It	**doesn't have to**	work.

6 **Complete the sentences with the correct form of** *(not) have to*.

1 I understand you aren't hungry. You *don't have to eat.* (not eat) it all.
2 My room is so messy. I .... (clean) it up.
3 There's a problem with my car. We .... (take) it to the garage.
4 The plane is leaving in an hour. He .... (not run).
5 Sarah already knows all the answers. She .... (not study) anymore.
6 It's your birthday on Sunday. We .... (invite) all your friends over.

7 **Work with a partner. Talk about what you have to do this afternoon.**

Listening

39 ① **Listen to the sketch "On Strike" and write the time expressions under the correct picture.**

later on Friday evening   Saturday morning   Friday evening

2 ....

1 ....

3 ....

40 ② **Listen again and choose the correct answers to the questions.**

1 Why do Simon and Sally go on strike?
  a Because they want more money.
  b Because there's too much work for them.
  c Because they don't want to go to school.

2 What does Sally say that she is not going to do?
  a Clean her room.
  b Take out the garbage.
  c Wash the dishes.

3 What does Simon say he is not going to do?
  a Wash the dishes.
  b Clean his room.
  c Do the vacuuming.

4 What do their parents think about the strike?
  a They don't mind.
  b They're angry.
  c They think it's funny.

5 What does Sally want her mom to do?
  a Help her with her homework.
  b Go shopping with her.
  c Make breakfast for her.

6 What does Simon want his dad to do?
  a Take him to his football game.
  b Play football with him.
  c Buy him some football cleats.

Reading

3 **Sam is at summer camp. Read his letter to his mom and place a check next to the correct pictures.**

Hi Mom,

[1] This camp is really great! There are a lot of things to do here. We can play different sports, like football and volleyball. We can go horseback riding. We can go swimming in the river—it's so fun! There are so many things to do. We never get bored.

[2] Yesterday I went on a canoeing trip! We went down the river in the canoes for two hours and then we had a picnic near the river. Jack, our guide, made a fire and we sang songs and played games. Then we went back to the camp by car. It was a great day.

[3] Tomorrow we're going to visit a car museum about 20 kilometers away. It has a great collection of cars from the last century. There are old Mustangs, Corvettes—everything. I'm definitely going to take my camera.

[4] Everything is great, but of course there are rules. We have to go to bed at ten o'clock. We have to help in the kitchen. We have to make our beds. But we don't have to do the dishes—that's good.

I hope you are good. I miss you. See you soon.

Love,

Sam

1 At the summer camp he can...

3 Tomorrow he's going to visit...

2 Yesterday he went...

4 He doesn't have to...

 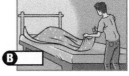

4 **Imagine you are going on the perfect vacation. Ask and answer questions with a partner and make plans.**

1 Where are you going to visit? (countries and cities)

2 What are you going to do there?

3 Who are you going to travel with?

4 How are you going to travel?

A Song 4 U Hey, let's travel, here we come!

5 Listen and sing.

Chorus
Hey, let's travel, here we come!
We want to see different places.
The world's exciting, and it's full
of different names and different faces.
So let's travel, here we come!

Let's take a trip to Honduras,
Belize, and Mexico.
Let's visit a lot of countries
and find a place to go.
Chorus

We're going to visit Chile,
Brazil, and Uruguay,
and we're going to enjoy it,
in sunshine or in rain!
Chorus

Writing for your Portfolio

6 Imagine you are at summer camp. Write a letter home to your family. Start like this:

> *Dear family, I'm having a great time at summer camp. Today we are going to ...*

Robots

Key words

robot	a machine	factory
intelligent machine	work automatically	put cars together
program	industrial robots	produce

1 **What is a robot?**

All robots are intelligent machines. They are made up of two elements:

1 They have a body.
2 When you program them, they work automatically.

2 **Read the text.**

ROBOT FACTS

Most robots today are industrial robots. Humans use them to make work easier and quicker. You often see them in car factories where they put the cars together. They are useful for this kind of work as it is "dull, dirty, and dangerous" (DDD). Robots are often used for DDD jobs and where a specific action needs to be repeated. It is very difficult for humans to do this.

There are many different kinds of robots. Some robots travel through space, work on the bottom of the ocean, or go inside volcanoes. They do the work of people, but for a different reason this time: these are places that are very dangerous for people, or impossible for people to go to.

Robots are everywhere. Most people don't know that robots help us every day and in many different ways. In most houses there are robots. For example, many washing machines are robots. People can program them and then they wash clothes automatically.

Some scientists make robots for fun. For example, the dog in the photograph to the right.

Japan produces the most robots. Every year in Japan's capital, Tokyo, there is a robot exhibition called Robodex. It is the largest robot exhibition in the world.

3 **Which of these are robots? Discuss in class.**

stoplight

DVD recorder

microwave

bicycle

MP3 player

car

pen

alarm clock

flashlight

dishwasher

> A dishwasher is a robot. We can program it and it works automatically.

> A flashlight is not a robot. We cannot program it to work automatically.

Mini-Project

4 **Take note of the machines you use during the day. Look up the English names of the machines in a dictionary. Decide if they are robots. Write a diary for your day.**

These are the machines I used during the day:

Date	Time	Object	Is it a robot?
May 23	7:00 a.m.	alarm clock	Yes
	7:50 a.m.	toaster	Not sure!
	8:30 a.m.	bus	....
	8:50 a.m.	stoplights	....
	9:00 a.m.	school bell	....
	1:00 p.m.	CD player	....
	2:30 p.m.	computer	....
	5:30 p.m.	automatic doors at supermarket	....
	7:30 p.m.	....	....

5 **Ask and answer questions about the results.**

Did you use … in the morning? / on the way to school? / at school? / … ?
Do you think a … is a robot?
How many robots did you use in the morning? / … / all day?

UNIT 6 Rules

In this unit

You learn
- *should/shouldn't*
- adverbs of manner
- words for school subjects

and then you can
- talk about shapes
- talk about school subjects
- talk about rules
- say how you do things

42 ● **1** Listen and read.

Harry I'm glad you're helping me with my math homework.

Fred Let's do it quickly. I still want to go out tonight.

Harry Triangles are no problem, but I don't understand how to do circles.

Fred Let me see. Ah, multiply these two figures here.

Harry Like this?

Fred No, don't do it so fast. You should think really carefully when you do math. Try again.

Harry OK, multiply, and then… finished. Great.

(Mrs. Elton comes in)

Mrs. Elton Hi, Fred. How's it going?

Fred Pretty good, Mrs. Elton, thank you.

Harry Yeah Mom, don't worry.

Mrs. Elton OK, Harry, but you should do your homework before you go out. *(Exits)*

Harry "You should do this, you shouldn't do that," I hate rules. Can you help me with my English homework, too, Fred?

Fred OK, but then we're definitely out of here!

2 **Circle T (True) or F (False) for the sentences below.**

1 Harry doesn't understand how to do triangles. T / F
2 Harry works too fast. T / F
3 Harry should finish his homework before he can go out. T / F
4 Fred is going to help Harry with his Spanish homework, too. T / F
5 Fred wants to go out. T / F

Get talking Talking about shapes

3 **Look at the picture below and say how many shapes there are.**

△	○	□	▭
triangle	circle	square	rectangle

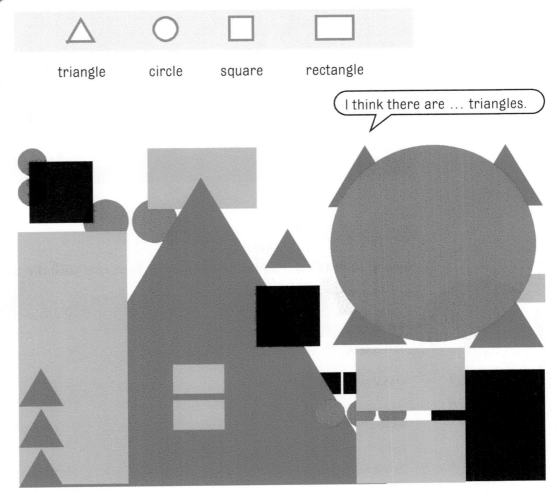

I think there are … triangles.

4 **Use your brain. Which shape is face down in the third picture?**

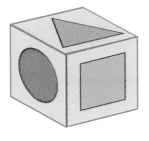 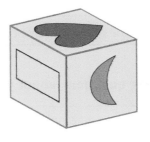 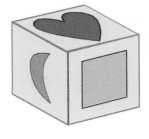

Language Focus

Vocabulary School subjects

 1 Listen and number the school subjects.

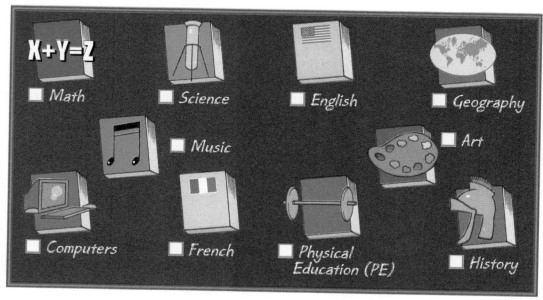

☐ Math   ☐ Science   ☐ English   ☐ Geography

☐ Music   ☐ Art

☐ Computers   ☐ French   ☐ Physical Education (PE)   ☐ History

Get talking Talking about school subjects

2 Here is Joshua's schedule. Complete the first row with the days of the week.

	Monday	1	2	3	Friday
9–9:55 a.m.	English	math	science	French	12 ....
10–10:55	4	English	8	science	French
			BREAK		
11:15–12:10	music	6	math	10	history
			LUNCH		
1–1:55 p.m.	math	science	9	English	13 ....
2–2:35	art	French		11	English
2:40–3:15	5	7		music	geography

 3 Listen and write in the missing subjects. Then work in pairs. Test each other.

A What class does Joshua have on Thursday mornings?   **B** He has…

4 Ask and answer questions about your own schedules.

A What do you have on Monday?   **B** I have …

Grammar

Should/shouldn't

1 **Look at the dialogue on page 54 and complete the examples.**

1 You .... really carefully.
2 You .... your homework before you go out.
3 "You .... do this, you .... do that." I hate rules.

We use **should** and **shouldn't** to talk about rules and what we are expected to do (or not do).
Should is the same for all subjects (**I/you/he** etc.). It is followed by the base form of the verb.

2 **Complete with *should* or *shouldn't*.**

1 You .... stop.
2 You .... be in bed by 11:00 p.m.
3 You .... walk on the grass.
4 You .... have a parent or guardian with you.
5 You .... park here.
6 You .... ride your bicycle here.

Sounds right

3 **Listen and repeat the chant below.**

45

I shouldn't go here and
I shouldn't go there!
Well, you shouldn't forget
that life isn't fair.

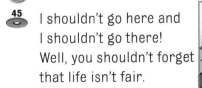

4 **Complete the dialogue with *should* or *shouldn't*.**

You shouldn't use all the paper!

Fred Mom, may I borrow your laptop?
Mom For how long?
Fred An hour?
Mom To do what?
Fred To check something on the Internet for school!
Mom Alright, but you ¹..................... put it back and you ²..................... go into my private files. And you ³..................... just surf the net; and you ⁴..................... print out everything you find. And you ⁵..................... turn it off before you put it back on my desk.
Fred Mom?
Mom Yes?
Fred Forget it.

Get talking Talking about rules

5 **Put the dialogue into the correct order. Listen and check. Then act it out.**

46

☐ **Dad** Alright, but before you go you should help me do the dishes.

☐ **Dad** OK, but you should be home by eight o'clock. You can't be late!

☐ **Dad** I don't care about the others.

☐ **Rory** But Dad. That's not fair. All the others stay out till 10.

☐ **Rory** But Dad, I just want to stay until 10.

1 **Rory** Dad, may I go to Sam's house tonight?

Adverbs of manner

6 **Put the words in the correct place, and then check them against the dialogue on page 54.**

> carefully   fast   quickly

Let's do it ¹.................
You should think really ².................
Don't do it so ³.................

We use adverbs to describe how to do things. We use adjectives to describe how things are.

adjective	adverb
quick	quick**ly**
slow	slow**ly**
careful	careful**ly**
bad	bad**ly**
easy	eas**ily**
happy	happ**ily**
angry	angr**ily**

Some adverbs are irregular:
good – **well**   fast – **fast**
She speaks Chinese really well.
Don't walk so fast.

7 **Write the correct adverbs under these adjectives.**

1 good ....

4 slow ....

2 fast ....

5 careful ....

3 angry ....

6 quiet ....

8 **Use the adverbs from Exercise 7 to complete the sentences.**

1 He plays football really .... He wants to play professionally.

2 The teacher shouted at us .... She wasn't happy.

3 Speak .... Henry's trying to sleep.

4 Don't walk so .... I'm in a hurry.

5 He drives really ....—more than 100kph sometimes.

6 You should do it .... It's very difficult and can be dangerous.

Get talking Saying how you do things

9 **Read the questionnaire below and check the boxes to say how you do things. Add your own adverbs if necessary.**

How do I ...?

- I always walk:
  □ pretty fast □ fast
  □ slowly   □ ....

- I speak:
  □ quickly   □ slowly   □ quietly
  □ loudly   □ ....

- I speak English:
  □ well   □ badly   □ easily
  □ slowly   □ ....

- I dance:
  □ well   □ badly   □ ....

- I always do my math homework:
  □ well   □ badly   □ easily
  □ slowly   □ ....

- I play volleyball:
  □ well   □ badly   □ ....

- I usually ride my bicycle:
  □ quickly   □ slowly   □ ....

10 **Now discuss your answers with a partner.**

A I always walk slowly.

B I don't. I always walk quickly. / So do I!

Skills

Reading

1 Read the text and complete the sentences below with *should* or *shouldn't*.

Hi, my name's Brittany and I want to go to drama school. But it's not easy! First you have an audition. My drama teacher and I chose my audition pieces very carefully, and I practiced them for months!

On the morning of the audition, I was very nervous. I spoke too fast, so they asked me to start again and to do it slowly.

In the afternoon, there was a dance, a singing, and an acting workshop. The dance workshop was difficult. The dance teacher taught us the steps really quickly. I did okay, I think. The singing workshop was easy because I can sing well. One girl sang badly, but she danced well. However, she didn't get into the school. To do that, you need to be a good singer and a good dancer.

When the letter came from the drama school, I opened it slowly... Guess what! I got in!

STELLA ★
DRAMA SCHOOL

★ ★ ★

To apply, you should:
be over 16 years old
be a good singer
★ dance well
★ be confident in front of
other people!

1 During the audition, you .... be nervous.

2 You .... prepare three audition pieces.

3 You .... choose your pieces carefully.

4 You .... practice your audition a lot.

5 You .... perform your audition too fast.

6 You .... learn the dance steps quickly.

7 You .... be a good singer and a good dancer.

Listening

47 **2** Listen to the dialogue between Laura and her younger sister Maria. Put a check next to the things Maria wants to borrow.

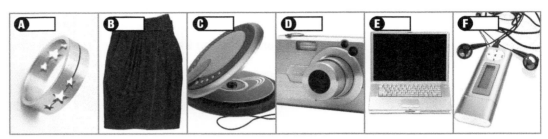

Get talking Borrowing things

3 Have a conversation with a partner.

A Can I borrow your tennis racket?

B OK, but you shouldn't lose it!

A Can I borrow your pen?

B Sorry, but I'm using it.

Writing for your Portfolio

4 Work in pairs. Write down eight things you *should* or *shouldn't* do at home. Some should be true, and some should be false. Read the sentences aloud. Your partner guesses which are true and which aren't.

I should make breakfast on Sundays.
I shouldn't eat in bed.

MORE fun with Fido

Fido, you shouldn't come in here.

Stop it, Fido. You shouldn't do that.

YOU SHOULDN'T SHOUT AT FIDO!

Check your progress Units 5 and 6

1 **Complete the names of the school subjects.**

1 m _ _ _   5 h _ _ _ _ _ _
2 sc _ _ _ _ _   6 F _ _ _ _ _
3 a _ _   7 m _ _ _ _
4 g _ _ _ _ _ _ _ | 7 |

2 **Complete the household verbs.**

1 c _ _ _ _ your r _ _ _
2 t_ _ _ out the g _ _ _ _ _ _
3 w _ _ _ the d _ _ _ _ _
4 m _ _ _ your b _ _
5 i _ _ _ the c _ _ _ _ _ _
6 c _ _ _ the d_ _ _ _ _ | 6 |

3 **Complete the dialogue with the correct form of *going to*.**

A What ¹....................... you .... (do) during spring break?

B I ²....................... (stay) at my cousin's house in Michigan.

A ³....................... you .... (be) there for a long time?

B I think I ⁴....................... (stay) for a week. | 4 |

4 **Complete the text about metro trains. Use *should* or *shouldn't*.**

When you travel on the metro, you ¹...................(no) eat or drink on the trains. You ²............. (yes) always have a ticket . You ³....................... (no) listen to music on your headphones so loudly that others can hear it. When a train arrives in the station, you ⁴....................... (yes) stand back. You also ⁵....................... (yes) be polite to staff. | 5 |

5 **Complete the dialogue with the correct adjective or adverb.**

A He works very ¹....................... (quick) and ²....................... (careful). I think he's going to be a good secretary.

B And he speaks English very ³....................... (good). In fact, his English is ⁴....................... (perfect).

A He drives very ⁵....................... (slow) and ⁶....................... (bad). He isn't a ⁷....................... (good) driver. Driving isn't ⁸....................... (easy) for him. | 8 |

6 **Complete the dialogue with the correct form of *going to*.**

A ¹....................... (you / help) John with his homework tonight?

B No, I ²....................... . I ³....................... (visit) my aunt.

A ⁴....................... (you / be) there all evening?

B Yes, I ⁵....................... . She ⁶....................... (give) me some old photos of the family.

A What ⁷....................... (you / do) on the weekend?

B I ⁸....................... (stay) home. I have a lot of homework to do.

A ⁹....................... (you / study) all weekend?

B Yes, I ¹⁰....................... . I have a big exam in two weeks! | 10 |

7 **Write five sentences about a school subject you *don't mind, like, love, hate,* and *sort of like*.** | 10 |

| TOTAL | 50 |

My progress so far is ...

:) great!   [ ]

:| good.   [ ]

:(poor.   [ ]

School life in the U.S.

1 Read about different methods of schooling in the United States.

The U.S. School System	
School	**Age**
Elementary school (Grades 1–8)	6–12
High school (Grades 9–12)	13–18

Homeschooling

In the United States, there are thousands of children who don't go to school at all, but learn at home instead. In 2000, 2 million children were "homeschooled."

The School System

Hi, my name's Susannah and I'm American. There are five kinds of schools in America: public schools, charter schools, private schools, religious schools, and homeschooling. I go to a charter school. Charter schools are run by a private organization and you don't pay. There are around 3,400 of these schools in America now.

Homeschooling

Hello, my name is Mark, and I have homeschooling. It's great! I do all my classes at home on the computer. I don't have to worry about what I'm wearing, and I don't have to catch the school bus. And of course I don't have homework after school!

The High School Prom

 48

2 Listen to Amy talk about her high school prom, and then answer the questions.

1 What did Amy wear to the prom?
2 Who asked her to the prom?
3 How did she travel to her date's house?
4 Was the tar on the driveway dry?
5 How much did her shoes cost?
6 How long did it take her mother to get the tar out of her hair?

3 **Over 2 U!** Choose one of the following activities:

a What is the school system like in your country? Write a short email to Susannah to explain.

b Compare homeschooling in America with school life in your country.

Homeschooling in America
Mark doesn't have to worry about what he is wearing.

School life in my country
I have to wear a uniform.

Do you know?

At an American high school, there is usually a junior and a senior prom.

The senior prom is at the end of the last year of high school.

Traditionally, boys dress in suits and ties and girls wear ball gowns.

The girl's date for the evening gives her flowers to wear.

MORE! Now you can watch Episode 3 of *Kids in NYC!* DVD

The school for magic

It's the first day at school for the young magicians.

Teacher Good evening.

Young magicians Hello!

Teacher Welcome to our school. On your first night I'm going to teach you …

Zak About how to do card tricks?

Teacher No, that's next week. Tonight you're going to learn how to make a stuffed animal disappear!

Jake And rabbits?

Teacher Well, yes, of course.

Dylan But we can't really make a rabbit disappear.

Teacher Of course you can't! You can only make it look like it disappeared.

Dylan Oh, right!

Brad Do we also learn how to do coin tricks?

Teacher Not this year. Maybe next year.

Emily What about guessing tricks?

Teacher That's next month.

Antonio I want to learn how to make my brother disappear.

Teacher Well, that wouldn't be very nice, would it, Antonio? Now, tonight you're just going to learn how to make a stuffed animal disappear.

Antonio Is it difficult to learn?

Teacher No, it's not difficult if you pay attention and follow my instructions closely.

Eva I can make money disappear.

Teacher I'm sure you can, Eva.

Young magicians Ha ha ha!

Teacher That's enough! Now, you have to watch closely. Don't say a word.

Felix Can I say "hocus-pocus?"

Teacher Aren't you listening? You must watch closely.

Eva Where did it go?

Teacher It's here, behind my back!

Young magicians But how did you do that?

Teacher Pay attention, you might learn a thing or two!

Young magicians Wow! This is going to be a little more tricky than we thought!

For **MORE!** Go to www.cambridge.org/elt/americanmore and take a quiz on this text.

In this unit

You learn
- time prepositions: *on, at, in*
- present continuous for future
- words for sports

and then you can
- make suggestions
- talk about sports
- talk about future plans

49 **1** **Listen and read.**

Harry What are you doing on Saturday, Olivia?

Olivia I think I'm going to a basketball game with Michael.

Sally Oh, we're going to Six Flags. Would you like to come along?

Olivia Six Flags? What's that?

Tony It's an amusement park. There are all kinds of different rides.

Harry …and there's a waterslide.

Olivia I don't really like amusement parks.

Tony Why not?

Olivia Too much standing around, so maybe some other time. Besides, this Saturday I'm watching the basketball game with Michael.

Harry Alright. So what are you doing on Sunday?

Olivia I'm not sure.

Harry Well, would you like to go to a movie with me? I could pick you up from your place at seven.

Olivia Oh, now I remember. I can't. I'm having dinner at Michael's place!

2 **Match the sentence halves.**

1 Tony, Sally, and Harry   a along because she doesn't like amusement parks.
2 Six Flags is an amusement   b go to the movies with Harry.
3 Olivia doesn't want to come   c at Michael's place.
4 On Saturday Olivia is   d watching a basketball game with Michael.
5 On Sunday Olivia can't   e are visiting Six Flags on Saturday.
6 She's having dinner   f park with great rides.

Get talking Making suggestions

50 **3** **Listen and number the pictures.**

 A
 B
 C
 D

51 **4** **Listen and repeat.**

A What are we doing this weekend?   **A** What are we doing on Sunday?
B Should we go to an amusement park?   **B** We could watch the last *Friends* season.
A Yes, why not?   **A** I'm not too interested in that.

5 **Work with a partner. Talk about the weekend. Use the pictures and the phrases below.**

Let's…
Why don't we…?
Should we…?
We could…

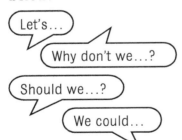
go for a walk

play tennis

sleep the whole time

go to a restaurant

go to the beach

Language Focus

Vocabulary Sports

52 **1** **Write the number of the sport in the picture. Then listen and check your work.**

play:	go:	
1 soccer	5 mountain climbing	9 skateboarding
2 tennis	6 cycling	10 swimming
3 basketball	7 mountain biking	11 surfing
4 volleyball	8 in-line skating	12 running

Get talking Talking about sports

2 **Work with a partner. Ask and answer questions about the sports in Exercise 1.**

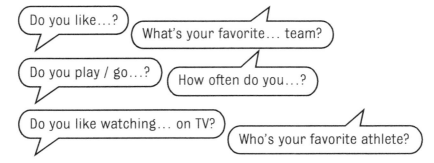

Do you like...?

What's your favorite... team?

Do you play / go...?

How often do you...?

Do you like watching... on TV?

Who's your favorite athlete?

Grammar

Time prepositions *on, at, in*

1 **Look at the examples and complete the rules.**

I was born **in** May.
I went to Colorado **in** 2006.
The movie starts **at** five o'clock.
On Monday we went to the library.
We went to the movies **on** May 23.

We use ¹........... with days of the week and the date.
We use ²........... with times.
We use ³........... with months and years.

(note, use **at** night, but **in** the morning/afternoon/evening)

2 **Fill in *on, at,* or *in*.**

1 .... Friday, April 17
2 .... Sunday
3 .... July

4 .... the morning
5 .... seven o'clock
6 .... Wednesday

7 .... the evening
8 .... night
9 1974

Present continuous *Future*

3 **Look at the dialogue on page 64 and complete the sentences with the days of the week.**

Olivia and Michael are watching a
   basketball game on ¹................
Sally is going to Six Flags on ²................

Harry is going to the movies on ³................
Olivia is having dinner with Michael on ⁴................

We can use the present continuous to talk about future arrangements.

4 **Complete the sentences with the present continuous form of the verbs below. Use short forms.**

leave	come back	sell
move	~~meet~~	stay

1 John*'s meeting* us in the city on Friday.
2 We ....
   to New York next year.
3 I ....
   home tonight.
4 They ....
   their house in November.
5 He ....
   school at the end of the year.
6 You ....
   from Japan on November 19.

5 **Make the following sentences negative.**

1 I'm coming to the party on Friday.
   I'm not coming to the party on Friday.
2 They are arriving in Florida on Monday.
   ....
3 You're watching the football game on
   Saturday..
   ....
4 We're buying her a present on Monday.
   ....
   ....
5 She's doing all her homework tonight.
   ....
   ....
6 He's playing in the next volleyball match.
   ....
   ....

6 Write questions and short answers.

1 you / play football / this afternoon (yes)

    A *Are you playing football this afternoon* ?
    B *Yes, I am.*

2 she / make soup / for lunch (no)

3 they / take a vacation / in August (no)

4 you / play video games / tonight (yes)

5 he / finish his work / tomorrow (no)

6 we / make breakfast / tomorrow
   morning (yes)

Get talking Talking about future plans

7 Complete the dialogue using the phrases below. Listen and check.

53

| I'm meeting | I'd love to | She didn't invite me | I'm watching |

Kevin What are you doing this weekend?

Dawn Well, ¹.. DVDs tomorrow night.
       Do you want to watch them with me?

Kevin ².. , but I can't.

Dawn Oh, why not?

Kevin ³.. Jenny. She's having a DVD party!

Dawn What? ⁴.. !

8 Read the table and put a check (✓) next to the things you are doing. Then complete
it for your partner.

	Me	My partner
• meet friends tomorrow	☐	☐
• stay home on Sunday	☐	☐
• play volleyball tomorrow	☐	☐
• do homework on Saturday	☐	☐
• go to the gym on Saturday	☐	☐
• go to a party on the weekend	☐	☐
• do homework tonight	☐	☐
• make dinner tomorrow	☐	☐
• play football on Saturday	☐	☐

Are you meeting friends tomorrow?

No, I'm not. I'm visiting my grandparents. What about you?

Skills

Reading

1 Read the magazine article and write the name, day, and time of day (morning, afternoon, or evening) under the pictures below.

1 _Greg, Saturday morning._

2 ....

3 ....

4 ....

5 ....

6 ....

What we do on the weekend

Greg

1 What time do you get up on weekends?

Greg On Saturdays I play soccer for the school team. The game starts at 9:00 a.m. On Sundays I stay in bed until about 10:00 a.m.

John I get up at 6 a.m. on Saturdays and Sundays because I have a paper route.

Wendy On Saturdays I get up late, about 10 a.m. On Sundays, if I go shopping I get up at 8 a.m. If I don't go, I get up about 9 a.m.

John

2 What do you usually do on Saturdays?

Greg Well, after lunch I sit and watch TV all afternoon. In the evening I usually hang out with my friends. We go to the movies or out to eat.

John I always do my homework on Saturday mornings. Then I know I have the rest of the weekend free. In the afternoon I go shopping with friends. In the evenings I stay home. But sometimes there's a party to go to.

Wendy In the morning I help my mom clean the house. But in the afternoon I usually go to a hockey game with my dad. We're big hockey fans, so we never miss a home game. In the evening I watch a DVD or go to a friend's house.

3 What do you usually do on Sundays?

Greg I don't do anything in the morning, but in the afternoon I go to the gym with my friends. In the evening I do my homework.

Wendy

John On Sundays I go fishing with my friends. We take a packed lunch and stay all day. In the evening I just relax.

Wendy Sometimes I go to the mall. I always have to find a few hours to do my homework, usually in the afternoons. In the evenings I listen to music.

Speaking

2 Work in pairs. Ask questions about the people in Exercise 1.

> What does Greg do on Saturday afternoons?

> Where does Wendy go on Sundays?

3 Put a check next to the activities that you do on the weekend and add two more. Then work with a partner and ask and answer questions.

What I do on the weekend

☐ play sports   ☐ watch sports   ☐ do homework
☐ get up late   ☐ watch TV   ☐ listen to music
☐ work   ☐ go to the movies   ☐ ....
☐ go shopping   ☐ go out to eat   ☐ ....
 ☐ go over to a friend's house

> Do you play a sport on the weekend?

> What sport do you play?

Sounds right /tʃ/

54 **4** Listen and repeat the chant.

Chicken, chicken,   Lots of **ch**icken,
eggs and **ch**eese.   lots of **ch**eese,
Some more rice?   and some rice.
Oh, yes, please!   Oh, that's nice!

Listening

55 **5** Listen to Fred and Annabel. Answer the questions.

1 What do they want to do?   2 When do they decide to do it?

56 **6** Listen again and complete the calendar using the words on the left.

do
  homework
go shopping
go to gym
aunt arrives
go to a football
  game
watch TV
help Dad
Sue's party

	Saturday	Sunday
morning		
afternoon		
evening		

	Saturday	Sunday
morning		
afternoon		
evening		

A Song 4 U Weekend

7 **Read and complete the song using the words on the left. Then listen and check.**

emails
late
always
Sunday night
classes
bed

It's the weekend. (x 4)

No more ¹......................... for a day or two.
It's the weekend. *(It's the weekend.)*
Stay in ²......................... all day—got nothing to do.
It's the weekend *(It's the weekend.)*
Get up ³......................... then you call a friend.
On the weekend *(On the weekend.)*
The computer's on, I've got ⁴......................... to send.
On the weekend *(On the weekend.)*

On the weekend. (x 4)

⁵......................... and it's over again.
End of the weekend. *(End of the weekend.)*
Goes too quickly, it's ⁶......................... the same.
End of the weekend. *(End of the weekend.)*

End of the weekend. (x 8)

Writing for your Portfolio

8 **Write answers to these questions.**

1 What time do you get up on the weekends?
2 What do you usually do on Saturdays?
3 What do you usually do on Sundays?

The feeling of happiness

1 Match the pictures below with some of the key words.

Where does HAPPINESS come from?

Happiness is the most wonderful feeling in the world. In fact, most people would like to be happy all the time. Where does happiness come from? And why is it so difficult to be happy? Read these texts and find out.

1 Thousands of years ago, life was very difficult and dangerous. There were a lot of wild animals, such as bears, mammoths, tigers, and wolves. People had to hunt these animals for food. That was dangerous, and not a lot of fun.

2 To motivate people to go hunting, the brain invented a trick: The feeling of happiness. When people hunted an animal and had something good to eat, their brain produced two chemicals, serotonin and endorphin. These chemicals make people feel happy. The brain also produced these chemicals when someone was the winner in a fight and when people spent time with friends.

3 Today, we no longer hunt such dangerous wild animals, but our brain still produces the same chemicals. For example, when we eat our favorite food, when we meet our friends, when we listen to our favorite music, when we do a good job at school, or when we play a sport and our team wins.

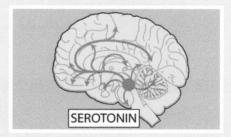

SEROTONIN

The bad news: We can't be happy all the time!

4 Let's look back thousands of years again. Imagine people sitting around a fire, eating a nice piece of tiger steak. Suddenly they hear something from behind a bush. Their brain produces another chemical, dopamine. Now the feeling is one of alarm! And their feeling of happiness was gone.

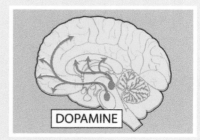

DOPAMINE

The good news: we can train our brain to be happy!

5 Experts say that you can train your brain to be happy. It is often small things that make us unhappy. It can help to try and think of positive things more often. Another good idea is to keep a happiness journal. Write three positive things in it every day. And before you fall asleep, think about what was good for you during the day.

Mini-Project Happiness

2 **Keep a happiness journal for one week. Then make a chart of your week.**

10 = extremely happy / 0 = not happy

My happiness log

Date: ....

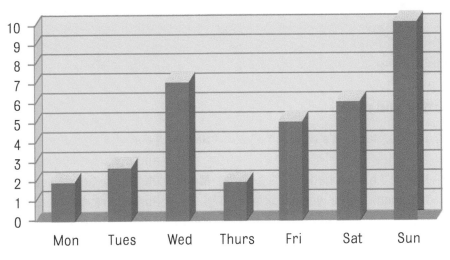

Last week was pretty good. I did something nice every day. On Monday I watched an interesting DVD about wildlife in Africa with my mom. On Wednesday my friends and I had a lot of fun at school. Thursday was not very good—I had a lot of homework! On Friday I did well in an English test. ;-) On Saturday my sister and I went to see our grandmother. We went for a walk with her dog. Sunday was great. It was my birthday!

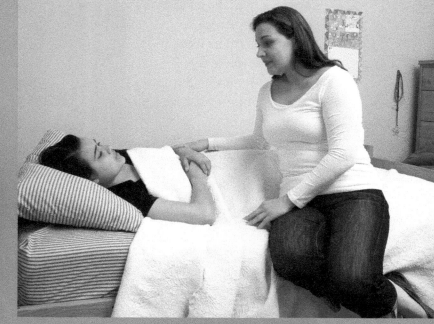

In this unit

You learn
- past continuous
- superlatives
- words for aches and pains

and then you can
- say what someone was doing
- talk about sickness

   1 **Listen and read.**

Mom Get up, Harry. It's time for school.

Harry I can't. I have a bad headache. I was working on my geography project until midnight. My head hurts.

Mom Should I get you a glass of water and some aspirin?

Harry Can I have two, please? It's the worst headache in the world.

Mom Alright. Let me go and wake up Sally first.

Mom Sally! Time to get up!

Sally I can't. I've got a sore throat and my stomach hurts.

Mom OK, Harry, here's your water. Sally's sick, too.

Harry Really? But she has a math test today.

Mom How interesting! She wasn't studying very much for it yesterday. Do you have a test today, too?

Harry Yes, but it's only a science test.

Mom This is the oldest trick in the book, Harry. Get out of bed now!

2 Complete the sentences from the dialogue.

What Harry says:

1 My head ....

2 I was working on ....

3 It's the worst headache ....

What Sally says:

1 I've got a sore throat and ....

What Mom says:

1 Should I get you a glass .... ?

2 Sally! Time to ....

3 Get out .... !

Get talking Saying what someone was doing

3 Listen and repeat.

A What was she doing at 7:00 p.m.?
B She was listening to music.

A What was he doing at 9:00 a.m.?
B He was taking a test.

4 Work with a partner. Ask and answer questions about the pictures.

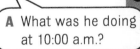

A What was he doing at 10:00 a.m.?

B He was reading a book.

Language Focus

Vocabulary Aches and pains

1 Match the pictures and expressions. Then listen and check.

☐ stomachache
☐ earache
☐ toothache
☐ backache
☐ a headache
☐ a cold
☐ a sore throat
☐ my knee hurts
☐ dizziness
☐ a broken ankle

Get talking Talking about sickness

2 Work in groups of three. Act out a problem and talk about it.

What's the matter with Jane?

Her knee hurts.

3 Complete the dialogues with the words on the left. Then practice using them with a partner.

hurt
broke
toothache
head

1 A Does your .... hurt?
  B Yes, I ran into a tree.

2 A What's the matter?
  B I .... my toe during the game yesterday.

3 A Why are you walking like that?
  B I .... my ankle when I was jogging.

4 A Where are you going?
  B To the dentist. I have a ....

Grammar

Past continuous Affirmative and negative

1 **Look at the dialogue on page 74 and complete the examples.**

I ¹................. .... on my geography project until midnight.
She ²................. .... very much for it yesterday.

We use the past continuous to talk about an action going on at a time in the past.

	Affirmative	Negative	
I/he/she/it	**was**	**wasn't**	sleep**ing** at six o'clock.
You/we/they	**were**	**weren't**	study**ing** for a test.

2 **Complete the sentences with *was / were* or *wasn't / weren't*.**

1 Jim ..was..... playing tennis at 10 a.m.
2 I .... speaking to my mom. It was my dad.
3 Paul and Wendy .... working.
4 She .... driving the car. I was!
5 We .... drinking lemonade. It was soda.
6 Yesterday afternoon, I .... watching a great show on TV.
7 My dad wasn't here on Saturday. He .... working at the office.

3 **Make the sentences negative.**

1 I was talking to Henry last night.
I ..wasn't.... talking to Henry last night.
2 We were shopping yesterday at 10:00 a.m.
....
3 They were studying in the evening.
....
4 He was having dinner at 7:00 p.m.
....
5 You were surfing the Internet this morning.
....
6 She was walking her dog last night.
....

Past continuous Questions and short answers

		Questions	Affirmative	Negative
Was	I/he/she/it	sleep**ing** at 6:00 a.m.?	Yes, I/he/she/it **was**.	No, I/he/she/it **wasn't**.
Were	you/we/they	study**ing** for a test?	Yes, you/we/they **were**.	No, you/we/they **weren't**.

4 **Write questions and short answers.**

1 you / play football / 8:00 p.m. (no)
Were you playing football at 8:00 p.m.?
No, I wasn't.
2 they / work / until 6:00 p.m. (no)
....
3 she / help / you (yes)
....

4 I / talk / to him (no)
....
5 it / rain / at 6:00 a.m. (no)
....
6 we / listen to / the teacher (yes)
....

Superlatives

5 **Look at the dialogue on page 74 and complete the examples.**

It's [1]................................. headache in the world.
This is [2]................................. trick in the book.

We use superlative adjectives to compare more than two things. The form depends on the adjective.

It's **the most** dangerous animal in the world.
His French is **the best** in the class. It's excellent.
It's **the worst** movie in the world. It's terrible.

a) If the adjective has one syllable,
   add [1].................................

b) Spelling: Some adjectives double the final letter, e.g. (**hot**) *It's **the** hot**test** day of the year*.

   If the adjective ends in —y, the letter y is replaced with [2]................., e.g. (**happy**) *It was **the** happ**iest** day of my life*.

c) With longer adjectives we use the words [3]................................. before the adjective.

d) The superlative of *good* is [4].................................,
   The superlative of *bad* is [5].................................

The bumble bee bat from Thailand is the smallest mammal in the world.

6 **Write the superlative form of these adjectives.**

1 strong   *strongest*.................................
2 sad   ....
3 lucky   ....
4 hot   ....
5 beautiful   ....
6 boring   ....
7 hungry   ....
8 good   ....
9 big   ....
10 romantic   ....
11 cold   ....
12 bad   ....

7 **Circle the correct word.**

1 It's *colder / coldest* than yesterday.
2 Yesterday was the *colder / coldest* day of the year.
3 She's the *more / most beautiful* actress in Hollywood.
4 I think this painting is *more / most beautiful* than the other one.
5 My bag is *heavier / heaviest* than yours.
6 What's in this bag! The *heavier / heaviest* book in the world?
7 She lives in the *bigger / biggest* house in the town.
8 My laptop is *bigger / biggest* than yours.

Skills

Reading

1 Read the text and answer the questions.

Save the rain forest!

The Amazon rain forest is one of the most important places on Earth. It produces more than 20 percent of the world's oxygen and is home to more than 2,000 medicinal plants, which help cure people who are sick. However, the rain forest is not safe. Every year people cut down many of the trees and the forest is getting smaller and smaller. About 500 years ago, more than 10 million native people lived in the Amazon rain forest. Today, there are fewer than 200,000. Native healers know all about the Amazon's important plants, but many of them are very old, and their environment is under attack. It is important for the world to know about these plants and to protect the Amazon rain forest so that native people can continue to live there.

1 Find two reasons in the text why the Amazon rain forest is important.
2 Who lives in the Amazon rain forest?
3 Why are these people important?

Listening

4 **2** Do the animal quiz, and then listen and check your answers.

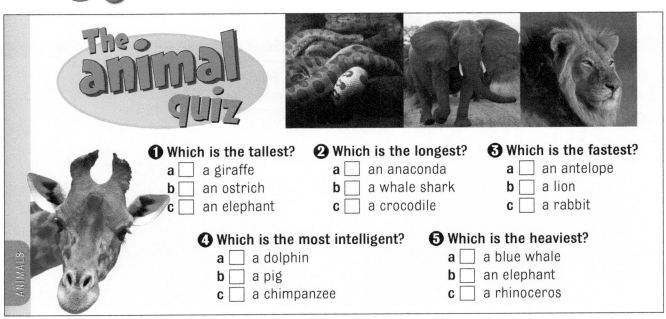

ANIMALS

The animal quiz

❶ Which is the tallest?
a ☐ a giraffe
b ☐ an ostrich
c ☐ an elephant

❷ Which is the longest?
a ☐ an anaconda
b ☐ a whale shark
c ☐ a crocodile

❸ Which is the fastest?
a ☐ an antelope
b ☐ a lion
c ☐ a rabbit

❹ Which is the most intelligent?
a ☐ a dolphin
b ☐ a pig
c ☐ a chimpanzee

❺ Which is the heaviest?
a ☐ a blue whale
b ☐ an elephant
c ☐ a rhinoceros

Writing for your Portfolio

3 **Read the letter and answer the questions.**

Dear Sally,

Miss Black told us about your accident. So you were riding a horse, you fell off, and you broke your ankle! That's terrible! And now you have to stay at home for three weeks. Three weeks with no school—poor you! But don't worry, Miss Black said she's going to send you a lot of homework.

The big news is that the school football team won the game yesterday. Now we're in the finals. The game's on Saturday, so think about us.

We all miss you. Get well and come back soon!
Your friends in English class

1 What's the name of the class teacher?
2 What happened to Sally?
3 How long is she going to be away from school?
4 What is the teacher going to send her?
5 What is the big news?

4 **Imagine one of your classmates is at home and can't come to school. Write him or her a letter. Think about the questions above to help you with ideas.**

MORE fun with Fido

Here, some chicken soup. This will make you better.

Poor Fido. He's not feeling well.

That's not what I wanted.

VETERINARY

Check your progress Units 7 and 8

1 Write the names of the sports.

1 .... 2 .... 3 ....

4 .... 5 .... 6 ....

☐ 6

2 Complete the words for sicknesses.

1 st _ _ _ _ _ ache   4 a c _ _ _
2 e _ _ ache   5 t _ _ _ _ ache
3 a s _ _ _ th _ _ _ _   6 to feel d _ _ _ _

☐ 6

3 Complete the dialogue using the correct form of the past continuous.

A What ¹...................... Sarah .... (do) last night?

B She ²...................... (work) at my house. We ³...................... (do) our homework together.

A ⁴...................... you .... (study) for the biology test?

B Yes, we ⁵...................... !

☐ 5

4 Complete the sentences with a time preposition.

1 .... Monday, I went to see my brother.
2 We went on vacation .... July last year.
3 The movie started .... 7:00 p.m.
4 I saw them .... night.
5 It began .... 1974.
6 I went swimming .... the morning.
7 We sleep .... night.
8 My birthday is .... November 1.

☐ 8

5 Complete the text with the superlative form.

The ¹................... (interesting) thing about me is my hair. It's red and curly and very long. Sometimes I think it's the ²................... (bad) hair in the world because it's always messy, but sometimes I think it's the ³................... (good) hair in the world because I look different and people talk to me a lot. I know this boy named Mark. He's the ⁴................... (tall) boy in school and the ⁵................... (intelligent). He always talks to me because he thinks my hair is great.

☐ 5

6 Complete the dialogue using the present continuous and the correct form of the verb *to be*.

A ¹...................... (you/go) to your cousin's house tomorrow?

B Yes, we ²...................... . We ³...................... (see) a movie.

A ⁴...................... (you/stay) there all weekend?

B No, we ⁵...................... . We ⁶...................... (go) to the country on Sunday.

A What ⁷...................... (you/do) there?

B We ⁸...................... (visit) my grandmother.

A ⁹...................... (she/meet) you at your cousin's?

B No, my aunt ¹⁰...................... (come) to get us.

☐ 10

7 Write five sentences about what you were doing at six o'clock last night and at eight o'clock this morning.

☐ 10

TOTAL ☐ 50

My progress so far is ...

😊 great! ☐

😐 good. ☐

☹ poor. ☐

Sports in the United States

1 Match the sport to the correct picture.

1 baseball
2 football
3 basketball

 **A**

 **B**

 **C**

2 Take the quiz, and then listen and check your answers.

An American SPORTS QUIZ!

Do YOU know?

Baseball is a mixture of the English games rounders and cricket, while football is a mixture of the games soccer and rugby.

1 Which sport is the oldest?
a football
b basketball
c baseball

2 Which sport do these terms come from: pitcher, home run, and pennant?
a baseball
b football
c rounders

3 There are... players in a baseball team.
a 9   b 11   c 13

4 The tallest basketball player is a Romanian, Gheorghe Muresan of the Washington Bullets. He is... .
a 2.31 m
b 2.20 m
c 2 m

5 What is a baseball field called?
a a star
b a diamond
c a square

6 The Cincinnati Red Stockings were the first professional ... team.
a basketball
b baseball
c football

7 How many points do you score for a touchdown in football?
a 5   b 6   c 1

3 Read and complete the table below.

My sports hero is Michael Jordan. He is the best basketball player in the history of the game. He joined the Chicago Bulls after he left college. The Chicago Bulls won three NBA championships with him on the team, and they had 72 wins in one season.

My sports hero is Joe DiMaggio. He was a famous baseball player. He died in 1999. He played for the New York Yankees. They won nine world championships with him on the team.

My sports hero is Joe Montana. He is a famous American football player. He was a quarterback for the San Francisco 49ers. His nickname is Joe Cool. In 1981, the 49ers won the NFC title with Joe on the team, and they defeated Cincinnati 26–21 in the Super Bowl.

NAME	TEAM	WINS
Joe DiMaggio	New York Yankees	Nine World Championships
		26–21 (against Cincinnati)
		3 NBA Championships

4  **Over 2 U!** Complete a table for your sports hero and write a short paragraph about that person.

 **MORE!** Now you can watch Episode 4 of *Kids in NYC!*

The world of *birds*
the biggest and the smallest

Ostriches

Ostriches are native to Africa, but they can live pretty much anywhere. They are the biggest birds in the world and normally are about 2.5 meters tall, so it isn't surprising that ostrich eggs are the biggest eggs in the world! An ostrich egg weighs about 1.6 kilograms, or about the same as 24 chicken eggs. In 1997, in Shanxi, China, an ostrich laid the heaviest egg in the world. It weighed 2.35 kilograms! The female ostrich sits on its egg in the daytime, and the male sits on it at night. The baby ostrich comes out of the egg after about 40 days.

Ostriches are also the fastest birds on land in the world. They can run at about 72 kilometers an hour. Ostriches are sometimes dangerous. They have very strong feet and can attack animals and people. Ostriches usually live between 50 and 75 years.

Bee hummingbirds

Bee hummingbirds live in Cuba. The males are the smallest birds in the world, while the female bee hummingbird is slightly bigger than the male. The male bee hummingbird weighs only 1.8 grams. That's lighter than a penny! The male is about five centimeters long.

When it is flying, the bee hummingbird moves its wings between 80 and 200 times every second. It has the highest body temperature of all birds in the world: about 40°C in the daytime, and about 20°C at night. Its body temperature goes down at night to save energy. Every day, a bee hummingbird eats about one gram of food (half its weight) and drinks about 15 grams of water (about eight times its weight!). Bee hummingbirds mostly eat insects and the nectar they get from flowers.

For **MORE!** Go to www.cambridge.org/elt/americanmore and take a quiz on this text.

In this unit

You learn
- past continuous vs. simple past
- *one/ones*
- quantity *a lot of, much, many*
- words for emotions

and then you can
- give reasons
- talk about emotions

6

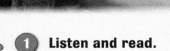 **1** **Listen and read.**

Tony Guess what just happened?

Sally What?

Tony I was walking down Maple Street when I saw two lights. They were on a huge silver thing that was blocking the street. Then a door opened and a lot of men came out. They were wearing silver clothing and had masks on their faces. The tallest one came up to me and said, "Why are you here?" I said, "I'm here because I live around here." But he asked me again, "Why are you here?" I wanted to run away, but the other ones blocked my path. The tall one said, "Send him away. There are not many more streets left and we haven't got much time."

Harry To do what? Catch people like you? What's this all about? Aliens?

Tony Maybe. They're still out there. Why don't you check?

(A minute later)

Harry Hilarious, Tony. Your aliens are people from the gas company, looking for a gas leak.

Tony Gotcha!

2 Put a check next to the correct answer.

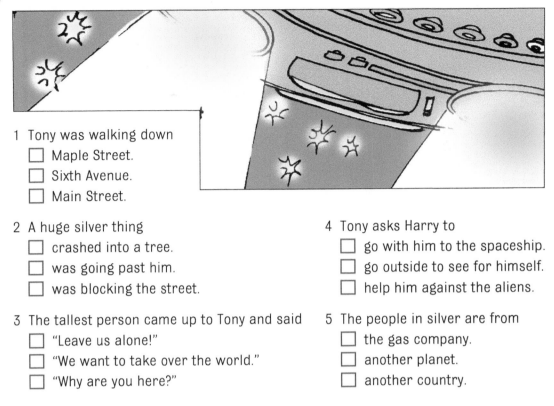

1 Tony was walking down
☐ Maple Street.
☐ Sixth Avenue.
☐ Main Street.

2 A huge silver thing
☐ crashed into a tree.
☐ was going past him.
☐ was blocking the street.

3 The tallest person came up to Tony and said
☐ "Leave us alone!"
☐ "We want to take over the world."
☐ "Why are you here?"

4 Tony asks Harry to
☐ go with him to the spaceship.
☐ go outside to see for himself.
☐ help him against the aliens.

5 The people in silver are from
☐ the gas company.
☐ another planet.
☐ another country.

Get talking Giving reasons

7 **3** Listen and repeat.

A Why weren't you at school?
B Because I had a cold.

A Why were you on the Internet for an hour?
B Because I had to answer 50 emails.

4 Match the questions and answers. Then work with a partner and act out the dialogues.

1 Why didn't you come to the park?
2 Why weren't you at Sue's party?
3 Why don't you watch the movie?
4 Why didn't you go swimming?

a Because it was too cold.
b Because I think it's boring.
c Because I was too tired.
d Because I had toothache.

Language Focus

Vocabulary Emotions

8 **1** Listen and write the number of the correct word on the left in the picture.

1 happy
2 nervous
3 shocked
4 surprised
5 scared
6 frightened
7 sad
8 thrilled
9 angry
10 bored

Get talking Talking about emotions

2 Work with a partner. Talk about how you feel in these situations:

> When I get a good score on a test, I feel happy.

- You get a good score on a test.
- You meet up with a friend after a long time.
- You win a lot of money.

- You listen to a long speech.
- You lose a game.
- You have an exam.

Grammar

Past continuous vs. simple past

1 **Complete the sentence below with the verbs in the correct tense. Check against the dialogue on page 84.**

I ¹.................................. down Maple Street when I ².................................. two lights. (walk/see)

A longer action (**past continuous**) is interrupted by a shorter one (**simple past**). They **were having** a picnic when they **heard** a noise.

2 **Circle the correct verb form.**

1 James *made / was making* coffee when we came into the kitchen.
2 When she broke her ankle she *played / was playing* volleyball.
3 Joanna *listened / was listening* to music when I came into her room.
4 I *rode / was riding* my bike when someone called my name.
5 When we *met / were meeting* her, she was crying.
6 When you *saw / were seeing* me, I was running.

3 **Complete the sentences with the past continuous and the simple past tense.**

1 When it s̲t̲a̲r̲t̲e̲d̲ to rain, I w̲a̲s̲ ̲w̲o̲r̲k̲i̲n̲g̲ in the yard. (start / work)
2 I .... a show on TV when he .... me. (watch / call)
3 They .... to Rita when I .... (talk / arrive)
4 When James .... , we .... dinner. (call / have)
5 Tamara .... emails when the lights .... out. (write /go)
6 I .... on the phone when I suddenly .... a loud noise. (talk / hear)
7 Kate and Rick .... when someone .... Kate's purse. (dance / steal)

They were having a picnic in the backyard when they heard a noise!

4 **Work with a partner. Ask her/him what she/he was doing at different times during the weekend.**

A What were you doing on Sunday at 3:00 p.m.?
B I was listening to music. What were you doing on Saturday at 8:00 p.m.?
A I was at the mall with my mom.

one / ones

5 **Look at the examples. Which words do *one* and *ones* replace?**

A Which boy are you talking about?
B The **one** with the black cap.

A Would you like the red or the blue sneakers?
B The red **ones** please.

6
9 **Complete the dialogue with the words below. Listen and check. Then act it out.**

large one	the blue one	one (x2)

Richard Dad? Can I have different T-shirt?
Dad Why? What's wrong with that ¹.................................. ?
Richard Nothing, but I want my extra ².................................. ;
³.................................. that has an alien's head on it.
Dad Sorry, I can't give you that ⁴..................................
Richard Why not?
Dad I washed it, and the water was too hot.
Now it's extra small!

Quantity *a lot of / much / many*

7 **Look at the examples and complete the rules below.**

There were **a lot of** men.   We don't have **much (a lot of)** time left.
There was **a lot of** rain in May.   There weren't **many (a lot of)** people at the concert.

1 We use ¹.................................. with count and noncount nouns in the affirmative and

negative form.

2 We use ².................................. with noncount nouns in the negative form.

3 We use ³.................................. with count nouns in the negative form.

8 **Complete the sentences with *much* or *many*.**

1 **A** Can you give me some money, please?
   B Sorry, I don't have .... myself.
2 When I was in Boston last Christmas, there wasn't .... snow.
3 John doesn't have .... friends.
4 My doctor says I shouldn't put .... salt on my food.

Skills

Reading

1 **Read the story.**

A NEW HOME PART 1

THE PRESIDENT OF TROJAN

The president of the planet Trojan was standing in front of her palace. She spoke to all the people.

"People of Trojan!" she said. "I have some bad news. Another planet is coming toward us. 100 years from now, the other planet is going to hit us and destroy us. There is nothing we can do."

The Trojan people were very scared. The president said more.

"Don't worry. We've got a plan. We're going to build spaceships, the biggest spaceships in the history of the universe. Each spaceship is going to carry 10,000 people, and we are going to build 20,000 spaceships! In this way, we can take every Trojan man, woman, and child to a safe place before the other planet hits us."

The people asked, "Where? Where is this safe place?"

The president said, "There is another planet, very far from here. It is a planet where Trojan people can live. The air is like our air, the water is like our water, and there is room

for us. The name of this planet is Earth!"

The next day, the people of Trojan started to build the spaceships. It took them a very long time (more than fifteen years) to build the first 1,000 spaceships. And after 50 years, 5,000 spaceships were ready. Finally, all 20,000 spaceships were ready. The spaceships were round, like huge soccer balls. They were so big that 10,000 Trojans could fit inside each one.

Then, one day, the people of Trojan said good-bye to their home. They got into their spaceships. And, one by one, the spaceships took off. The Trojans began the journey to their new home.

20 years later, the spaceships landed on the planet Earth.

2 **Match the sentence halves.**

1 Another planet was going to...

2 The Trojan people planned...

3 The Trojan people built...

4 10,000 Trojan people went...

5 After 20 years, the Trojan people landed...

a into each spaceship.

b 20,000 very big spaceships.

c hit the planet Trojan.

d on planet Earth.

e to travel to Earth.

Listening

  3 **Listen to the end of the story and put the pictures in order.**

4 **Listen again and choose the correct answers.**

1 Jenny's dog barked
  because he saw:
  a strange yellow seeds.
  b a cat.
  c Jenny's father.

2 Jenny's father thought
  the seeds were:
  a strange.
  b beautiful.
  c dirty.

3 Jenny put the seeds:
  a in the house.
  b in her father's car.
  c in the garbage can.

Speaking and listening

5 **Work in pairs. Use the words and pictures to tell the story.**

key
a strange
  green light
a strange noise
lock
turn around
pick up

6 **Listen to the story.**

Reading and speaking

7 Here are two possibilities for the next part of the story. Choose which one you like best and say why.

A

He saw a chair and he sat down. It was very comfortable! Then he found a button on the floor, near the chair. "What's this?" he said, and he pushed the button. The chair started to go around and around very quickly, but after a minute it stopped. James went out of the house. He was in the year 2090!

B

He saw a chair and he sat down. It was very comfortable! He went to sleep.

Five hours later, James woke up. In front of him were two strange people with pink eyes. "Why are you here?" said one of the strange people. "You shouldn't be here! Now we have to take you to our planet!"

I like the first one better because it's…

Writing for your Portfolio

8 Write your own end to the story.

He saw a chair and he sat down…

9 Work in groups of four. Tell your stories and decide whose story you like best.

MORE fun with **Fido**

How strange!

He usually comes in the afternoon.

Good morning, Fido.

Famous modern authors for teenagers

1   Read the fact files about three famous authors who write for teenagers.

FACT FILE

Name: Jacqueline Wilson
Born: 1945, Bath, England.
Other jobs before writing: Journalist
Wrote first novel: 1954 (aged nine)
Famous novels: *Double Act, Vicky Angel, Girls in Love, Tracy Beaker.*
Interesting fact: She has more than 15,000 books in her house!

FACT FILE

Name: Eoin Colfer
Born: 1965, Wexford, Ireland.
Other jobs before writing: Elementary school teacher
Wrote first novel: 1999
Famous novels: *Benny and Omar, Artemis Fowl.*
Interesting fact: He has worked in Saudi Arabia, Tunisia, and Italy.

FACT FILE

Name: Jerry Spinelli
Born: 1941, Pennsylvania, USA
Other jobs before writing: Editor
Wrote first novel: 1982
Famous novels: *Maniac Magee*
Interesting fact: He wanted to be a baseball player. When he was 16, he wrote a poem about a football game. His local newspaper published it!

2 **Read the summaries of three novels. Which book would you like to read?**

Vicky Angel **by Jacqueline Wilson**
Jade and Vicky have been best friends since kindergarten. One day
the two girls argue. The same day Vicky gets killed by a car. Jade
cannot forget Vicky. She tries to make new friends. But one day
Vicky appears again as a ghost. Jade is happy, but other people see
that she's talking to herself and they think she's crazy. Jade goes
and sees a psychologist who helps her to find out who she really is.

Maniac Magee **by Jerry Spinelli**
Jeffrey "Maniac" Magee is a young white boy whose parents die
in an accident. Jeffrey starts to live with his aunt and uncle, but
he soon runs away from home and lives for some time in a zoo.
Then a black family takes him in. Jeffrey soon finds out that there
is a problem. In the town there are black people who live
in the East End and white people who live in the West End.
Jeffrey doesn't understand why the blacks and whites do not like
each other. He travels throughout the town and tries to
change how the people think.

Artemis Fowl **by Eoin Colfer**
Artemis Fowl is 12 years old. The Fowls are an old Irish family.
Artemis wants to get rich. He finds out that fairies and elves exist
and that they have magical books. He plans to get one. He hopes
that the book will show him how to get the gold treasure of the
fairies. With the help of his butler he tricks an old fairy woman.
She lends him her magical book but only for 30 minutes. Artemis
scans it with a digital camera and emails it to his computer. He
tries to find out about the treasure of the fairies. But he needs
help so he kidnaps an elf. A big fight begins.

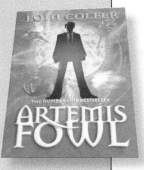

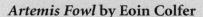

(I think … sounds interesting/boring/funny.)   (I like /don't like stories about …)

Mini-Project Authors and books

3

Either
Check the Internet or the library to
discover facts about a writer for teens.

Scott Westerfeld is an American
science fiction writer. His books are
for young adults...

Or
Write a short summary of a book
that you have read and enjoyed.

A book that I really enjoyed was
The Catcher in the Rye by J.D.
Salinger. It was published in 1951. It
tells the story of a 16-year-old boy
named Holden Caulfield...

Shouldn't we ask?

In this unit

You learn

- should/shouldn't
- conjunctions: and/so/but/because
- words for directions and places

and then you can

- use large numbers
- give advice
- ask for and give directions

---

13 **1** **Listen and read.**

Sally Let's ask someone again.

Harry No way! I hate asking for directions. Let me look at the map.

Olivia Come on. Shouldn't we ask? We're lost.

Harry We're not. I can figure this out.

Sally Look. I'll give you one minute to figure it out because I'm getting really tired.

Harry OK. We're here at the corner of Market Street and Cooper Lane. If we turn right at the end of Cooper Lane and then take the second left, we are close to the gas station.

Sally Yes, there's the gas station on the map. And from there?

Olivia I think we should ask somebody <u>now</u>.

Harry Hang on. From the gas station we walk straight on as far as the post office. There we turn left again. And then... we're lost again, so, let's start over.

Olivia Let's ask someone!

Sally Excuse me, where's the movie theater?

Officer Just cross the street and turn right. It's there!

Sally Thanks! Come on Harry!

2 **Circle T (True) or F (False) for the sentences below.**

1 Harry wants to look at the map. T / F
2 Olivia wants to ask for directions. T / F
3 They are at the corner of Cooper Lane and Main Street. T / F
4 Harry says they have to go to the end of Cooper Lane. T / F
5 They're looking for the post office. T / F
6 The movie theater is very close. T / F

Get talking Using large numbers

3 **Listen and repeat.**

100 one hundred
1,000 one thousand
100,000 one hundred thousand
1,000,000 one million

8,347 eight thousand, three hundred, and forty-seven
47,222 forty-seven thousand, two hundred, and twenty-two
721,877 seven hundred and twenty-one thousand, eight hundred, and seventy-seven

4 **Now say these numbers. Then listen and check.**

9,341   52,304   72,605   823,988   1,000,732

5 **Work with a partner. Use the picture and talk about saving money.**

$ 1,204 Jane
$ 22,187 Sam
$ 672,344 Mike
$ 1,000,892 Sue
$ 3,001,299 Claire

A How much did Jane save this year?

B She saved $1,204.

Language Focus

Vocabulary Directions and places

16 **1** **Listen and repeat.**

go straight ahead

turn left

turn right

take the second right

take the first left

go past the...

cross the...

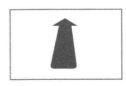
go as far as the...

17 **2** **Match the places to the correct numbers. Then listen and check.**

☐ gas station
☐ parking lot
☐ school
☐ post office
☐ tourist office
☐ bank
☐ hospital
☐ movie theater
☐ grocery store
☐ restaurant
☐ hotel

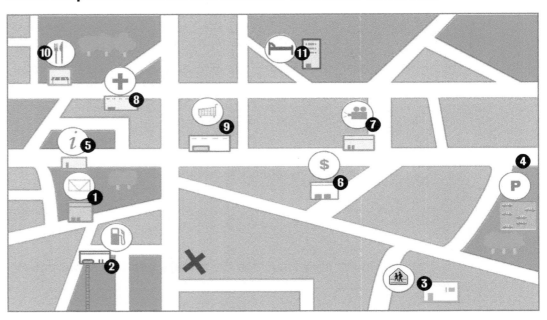

Get talking Asking for and giving directions

18 **3** **Listen and repeat.**

A Where's the post office?
B Go straight ahead and take the second left.

A How do I get to a gas station?
B Go straight ahead and take the first left.

4 **Work with a partner. Choose different places from Exercise 2 and give directions from X.**

Grammar

Should/shouldn't

1 **Look at the dialogue on page 94 and complete the examples.**

I think we ¹.................................... ask someone now.
².................................... we ask?

We use **should** and **shouldn't** to give advice and to say what we think is a good idea.
Should is the same for all subjects (**I/you/he** etc.). It is followed by the base form of the verb.

2 **Match the sentences to make dialogues.**

1 I'm tired.
2 I have a headache.
3 My teacher's angry with me.
4 My cat's sick.
5 It's raining outside.
6 It's a dangerous part of town.

a You shouldn't talk in class.
b You should take it to the vet.
c You should take an umbrella.
d You shouldn't go there alone.
e You shouldn't go to bed so late.
f You should take an aspirin.

3 **Complete the sentences with should or shouldn't.**

1 **A** I don't feel very well.
   B You .... go to bed.

2 **A** We're bored.
   B You .... watch so much TV.

3 **A** There's a new girl at school named Gillian.
   B You .... invite her to our barbecue.

4 **A** I don't understand my math homework.
   B You .... ask your teacher to explain it again.

5 **A** I can't fall asleep at night.
   B You .... drink so much caffeine.

6 **A** I don't have any money.
   B You .... buy so much music.

7 **A** I'm going to live in Brazil for a year.
   B You .... learn some Portuguese.

8 **A** I failed my science test.
   B You .... study more.

4 **Work in pairs. Say what these people should and shouldn't do. Use the words below.**

| clean his room | do his homework | call a friend | listen to music |
| talk on his cell phone | rent a DVD | watch TV | read |

Conjunctions *and / so / but / because*

(5) Match the sentence halves.

I know the store is on King Street, **but**	I'm getting really tired.
Just cross the street **and**	I can't find it at the moment.
And then ... we're lost again, **so**	turn right.
I'll give you one minute to figure it out **because**	let's start over.

(6) Match the sentence halves.

1 I looked for the key,
2 My friends were sick
3 I got a high score on the test
4 The movie started at 10,
5 She likes you a lot
6 I had no money,

a and had to stay at home.
b because I had studied really hard.
c so we couldn't be home by 11 o'clock.
d so I couldn't buy anything.
e but I couldn't find it.
f because she thinks you are so smart.

They wanted to go swimming, but it was too cold!

(7) Complete the dialogue in the sentences below. Listen and check, and then act the dialogue out.

19

she gave us directions	we went home
they were for the wrong theater	we couldn't find the theater

Dana Hi Jim, did you enjoy the movie last night?

Jim We didn't see it because ¹...

Dana Why didn't you ask someone the way?

Jim Well, we asked someone and ²...

Dana So what was the problem?

Jim She gave us directions, but ³...

Dana The wrong theater? What did you do?

Jim We didn't want to see the movie that was on there, so ⁴...

Skills

Reading

1 Read the dialogues and write the letter of the correct building in the signs.

Post office

Restaurant

Library

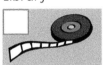

Movie theater

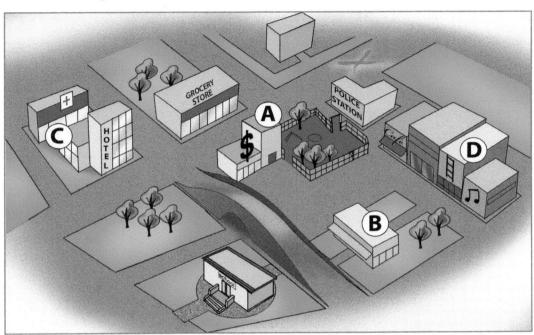

Dialogue 1:

Woman Excuse me, where's the post office?

Man Go straight ahead as far as the grocery store. Then turn left. On the corner, there's a large bank. The post office is next to the bank.

Woman Thank you.

Man You're welcome.

Dialogue 2:

Boy Excuse me. Can you tell me where the movie theater is?

Woman The theater? It's on Hill Street.

Boy How do I get there?

Woman Go straight ahead, take the first left, and go past the police station. You'll see a little park in front of you. Go past the park and straight ahead and the theater is next door to a large music shop.

Boy Thank you.

Woman No problem.

Listening

 20 **2** Listen to two more dialogues and write the letters of the other two buildings on the signs.

A Song 4 U **Looking for Liz**

3 Listen and complete the song with the words on the left.

went
know
go
far
name
see
stop
laughed

Chorus
Young man:
I'm looking for my friend,
I don't ¹ .... where she is.
I'm looking for my friend,
she has blonde hair, her ² .... is Liz.

Excuse me, sir,
Did you ³ .... her?
Where did she ⁴ .... ?
I have to know.

Man 1:
She ⁵ .... along Main Street,
and turned right at the store.
She went as ⁶ .... as Town Square
And there I saw her stop.

Chorus

Man 1:
I saw her ⁷ .... at Town Square.
I saw a young man wait for her.
They talked. They ⁸ ....
They said goodbye.

Young man:
Can I still catch her?

Man 1:
You can try.

Writing for your Portfolio

4 Write a similar email with directions from school to your house.

To: Josh **From:** Sally	**Re:** Directions to my house

Go straight ahead from the school. Take the first right and then the second left and that's my street, 104th Street. I'm at 3955.

Check your progress Units 9 and 10

1 **Complete the words about emotions.**

1 When I gave my presentation, I was very
n _ _ _ _ _ _.
2 I was sh _ _ _ _ _ when I failed the
test.
3 He was t _ _ _ _ _ _ _ _ when he won the
race.
4 They were a _ _ _ _ when they lost all their
money.
5 She was s _ _ _ _ _ _ to be in the house all
alone.
6 I was s _ _ _ _ _ _ _ _ when she didn't
come.　　　　　　　　　　　　　　　　6

2 **Write the direction words.**

| ↑ | ↰ | ⇑ |

1 .... 2 .... 3 ....
....

| ↱ | ↑ | ↩ |

4 .... 5 .... 6 ....
....
　　　　　　　　　　　　　　　　　　　　　　　　6

3 **Complete the text. Use the simple past or
the past continuous.**

I ¹...................... (walk) down the street
yesterday when I ²......................(hear) a
strange noise. I ³...................... (look) down and
⁴......................(see) a strange green man. He
⁵...................... (run) down the street in front of
me. "Stop!" I ⁶...................... (shout). He didn't
hear me, so I ⁷......................(run) after him
into the park. In front of me there was a big
crowd of small yellow people. They ⁸......................
(talk) and ⁹...................... (dance). I ¹⁰......................
(start) to dance, too! Suddenly, a loud voice
said, "Wake up Tom!" I ¹¹...................... (open)
my eyes and my friend Sam ¹²......................
(stand) next to me. "You ¹³......................
(dance) in your sleep!" he said.　　　　13

4 **Complete the sentences with *a lot of,
much,* or *many.***

1 This room is very dark. There isn't ....
light in it.
2 There wasn't .... time.
3 There weren't .... things to do there.
4 There was .... traffic this morning. It
was terrible!
5 There weren't .... books in the store.
　　　　　　　　　　　　　　　　　　　　　　5

5 **Complete the sentences with *and, so, but,*
or *because.***

1 I didn't feel well, ... I stayed at home.
2 He liked her .... she was happy.
3 I went to Spain, ... I wanted to go home.
4 She likes swimming .... jogging.
5 We were late .... there was an accident.
　　　　　　　　　　　　　　　　　　　　　　5

6 **Complete with *the one* or *the ones.***

A Can I try on those jeans?
B ¹.............. in the window?
A No, ².............. here. Oh, and that T-shirt, too.
B ³.............. near the window?
A No, ⁴.............. over there.
B Sure! Those jeans are nice, too. ⁵..............
with the silver stars.　　　　　　　　　5

7 **Write advice for a friend who is
bored / not ready / nervous about an exam
or sad / angry with his / her parents.**

　　　　　　　　　　　　　　　　　　　　　10
　　　　　　　　　　　　　　　TOTAL　　50

My progress so far is ...

😊 great!　　　　　　　　　　☐

😐 good.　　　　　　　　　　☐

☹ poor.　　　　　　　　　　☐

The history of the car

1 **Read about the history of the car.**

In the 1700s, a Frenchman named Antoine de la Mothe Cadillac went to the United States and founded the city of Detroit. Many years later, in 1902, an engineer named his car after the Frenchman. The famous Cadillac is still a very popular car today.

In 1896, Henry Ford built the first American gas-powered car in Detroit. He called it the Quadricycle because it was made with four bicycle wheels. He also produced the first cheap car there, the Model T Ford. In the same year, William Durrant founded General Motors, and Detroit became the Motor City of America.

2 **Match the cars with the model.**

1 Cadillac   2 Model T   3 Mustang

22 **3** **Which car is it? Guess the answers. Then listen and check.**

Silver Ghost   Fiat   Ferrari

1 The first .... was built in 1899 in Italy. Its top speed was 35 kilometers per hour. Only 25 of them were produced.

2 From 1906 until 1922 there was one model of this luxury car. It was the .... The owner of this company loved flying. He died in a plane crash in 1910, before his cars became successful.

3 The owner of this company was a racing driver and the first .... was a racing car. Later, in 1948, the company built the first sports car for the road.

Do you know?

The earliest cars were very uncomfortable. The driver's seat and the front seat of the car was a hard bench.

Cars were definitely not fast. In 1898, the New York City Police Department chased speeding motorists on bicycles.

In the early 1900s when Henry Ford produced the first gas-powered cars in the United States, there was only one color, BLACK.

4  **Find out about a kind of car that you like. Write a brief description of it and its history.**

MORE! Now you can watch Episode 5 of *Kids in NYC!*

Learn MORE about Culture

Looking for Keiko

Last year a Japanese girl stayed at our house. Her name was Keiko, and she was here with her classmates and her English teacher.

Keiko was not very good at finding her way around so Dad took her everywhere in the car. One day he didn't have time, so he asked me to meet Keiko at school, but I forgot.

I was in my room when the phone rang. It was Keiko. "Hello" she said, "I am lost. I don't know where I am. Can you help me?"

I was in trouble! I could hear Dad saying, "What did I tell you, George? Go and meet Keiko at school! No video games for the rest of the week, young man!"

"Of course!" I said. "Where are you?"

"I don't know," she said. "There are a lot of gray houses, and they all look the same. And there's a bus stop at the end of the street."

"Keiko," I said. "Listen. What's the name of the street?"

"I don't know. I can't see a street sign."

"Walk to the corner, Keiko," I said. "There should be a sign."

"Oh, yes, I can see it. Hello? My battery's low."

"Keiko," I shouted. "Just tell me the name of the street. And stay where you are!"

"Yes, the name of the street is very long. It's …"

Just then there was a click. I couldn't believe it!

I put on my jacket and got my bike. I thought, "She walked from the school, so maybe she walked in this direction from there."

I went back to the school and then followed the main route back to my house. Half an hour later there was still no Keiko. I rode my bike back home. I went up and down some smaller roads. Still no Keiko.

About 200 meters away from my house, there's a street up a long hill. I didn't want to go up that street, but then I thought: "OK, I may as well..." I turned onto the street. Then I checked out the side streets. First left—nothing. Second, third, fourth left—nothing. I was so tired. First right—and just 100 meters away, there was Keiko. I waved and called her name. She saw and ran up to me. She was so happy to see me.

I was happy to see her, too!

For **MORE!** Go to www.cambridge.org/elt/americanmore and do a quiz on this text.

In this unit

You learn
- *will/ won't*
- *might/might not*
- words for the weather

and then you can
- make excuses
- talk about the weather

23 **(1)** **Listen and read.**

Sally   Hi, Fred. It's Sally! We're going to the beach this afternoon. Would you like to come?

Fred   I'm not sure. I think it might rain.

Sally   Really? Look outside—the sky's blue, there aren't any clouds, and there's not even a breeze. It won't rain. No way!

Fred   OK, I'll be there in 10 minutes.

(Harry comes in)

Harry   Who was that?

Sally   Fred. He'll be here in 10 minutes. He thinks going to the beach might not be a good idea. It might rain!

(10 minutes later)

Fred   Are you sure you want to go to the beach?

Sally   Of course. It'll be hot and sunny for the rest of the day.

Fred   Too hot! I think there might be a thunderstorm. Why don't we stay here and watch a DVD?

Sally   Oh Fred, not again! I don't want to watch DVDs three times a week.

2 **Circle T (True) or F (False) for the sentences below.**

1 Sally and Harry want to go to the beach in the afternoon. T / F
2 Fred thinks it might rain. T / F
3 There are some clouds in the sky. T / F
4 Sally thinks the weather will be good for the rest of the day. T / F
5 Fred thinks there might be a thunderstorm. T / F
6 Sally wants to watch a DVD. T / F

Get talking Making excuses

24 **3** **Listen and number.**

4 **Work with a partner and match the phrases. Then make dialogues.**

1 Let's go to the park.
2 Let's ride our bikes.
3 Let's go to a movie.
4 Let's go skateboarding.
5 Let's go and buy some candy.

a No, there might be a lot of people there.
b No, there might not be any tickets left.
c No, I might get a toothache.
d No, it might rain soon.
e No, I might get hurt.

Language Focus

Vocabulary Weather words

25 **1** **Write the correct numbers in the pictures. Then listen and check.**

1 sunny	3 rainy / showers	5 snowy	7 thunderstorms	9 cold
2 windy	4 cloudy	6 foggy	8 hot	

   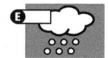

  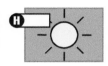 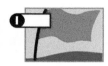

Get talking Talking about the weather

26 **2** **Listen and repeat.**

A What's the weather like in Seattle?
B It's very rainy and windy.

A What's the weather like in Boston?
B It's foggy and cold and only 12°C.

3 **Work with a partner. Take turns to describe the weather and guess the place.**

A It's very windy and rainy here and only 14°C.

B You're in Seattle.

Seattle	☁	⚑	14°C
Phoenix	🌡	☀	30°C
Minneapolis	☁	〰	-10°C
New York City	⚑	☀	16°C
Kansas City	⛈	☁	16°C
Denver	🌡	☁	0°C
San Francisco	☀	⚑	20°C

Grammar

Will / won't

There'll be some light showers later.

1 **Look at the dialogue on page 104 and complete the examples.**

He ¹......... be here in 10 minutes.
It ².................... rain. No way!
I ³.................... be there in 10 minutes.

We use **will** and **won't** for expectation, hopes, and predictions for the future.
Will and **won't** are the same for all subjects (**I/you/he,** etc.). They are followed by the base form of the verb.
We **will meet** again. (We**'ll meet** again.)
I **will not be** away for a very long time. (I **won't be** away for a very long time.)

We also use the *will* future when we spontaneously make a decision, promise, or offer.
Maybe **I'll try** cooking, too.
I'll help you with your homework tonight.

2 **Put the words in the correct order to make sentences. Use short forms.**

1 it / rain / I / tomorrow / think / will
   I think it'll rain tomorrow.

2 soon / sister / car/ buy / will / a / my
   ....

3 thunderstorm / be / this / will not /
   afternoon / a / there /
   ....

4 win / race / will not / you / the /
   ....

5 they / year / will / go / to New York / next
   ....

6 year / move / he / next / will / house
   ....

7 you / I / shopping / go / will / for
   ....

8 will not / much / time / I / have
   ....

Will Questions and short answers

Questions	**Will** I / you / she / he / it / we / you / they be famous?
Short answers	Yes, I / you / she / he / it / we / you / they **will**.
	No, I / you / she / he / it / we / you / they **won't**.

3 **Write questions for these answers.**

1 No, my friends won't go to the beach
   tomorrow.
   Will your friends go to the beach
   tomorrow.....?

2 Yes, the sun will come out soon.
   ....?

3 Yes, I will be here later.
   ....?

4 Yes, we will stay here for the weekend.
   ....?

5 No, they won't go out tonight.
   ....?

Might / might not

4 **Complete the examples with the missing words. Then check against the dialogue on page 104.**

He thinks going to the beach ¹.................. .... be a good idea.
I think there ².......... be a thunderstorm.

We use **might** and **might not** to talk about possibility or uncertainty in the future.
Might is the same for all subjects (**I/you/he,** etc.). It is followed by the base form of the verb.

5 **Complete with *might* or *might not*.**

1 I'm tired. I *might.* go to bed early tonight.
2 He left the office very late, so he .... be home for dinner.
3 There are a lot of clouds in the sky, so it .... rain later.
4 She didn't pass her test, so she .... be very happy.
5 They're a good team. They .... win the championship this year.

6 **Read the story. Complete the speech bubbles with the numbers of the correct phrases.**

1 I have too much to do.
2 The test has been postponed.
3 We might get home too late.
4 We're going to a movie.

William the Worrier

William has a science test in the morning, but he's worried. William is always worried!

☐ ...... Do you want to come?

No thanks. ☐ ...... And I have to get to bed early tonight.

Time to come to the dinner table.

The next morning.

☐ .... I'll eat while I study!

I'm sorry, William. ☐ ......!

7 **Read William's worries. Work with a partner and think of his reasons to worry.**

1 I don't want to go to the beach. It might be too hot.
2 I don't want to go skiing. ....
3 I don't want to go near that dog. ....

Skills

C [ ]

Reading

1 Read and match the texts to the correct photo.

A [ ]

B [ ]

D [ ]

1 Jo

Last year, I went on vacation in California. We visited Joshua Tree National Park. We went in May and it was very HOT! There were some strange rock formations. They were like nothing I'd ever seen before. There were also the most amazing trees. They are the Joshua trees after which the park is named.

2 Juan

I went to Las Vegas, Nevada, last summer and it was very, very hot. There were never any clouds in the sky! It was more than 30 degrees every day until about 8:00 p.m.! I liked it, but this summer I think we'll go somewhere different —somewhere a little colder!

3 Mel

To me, the Boundary Waters that lie between the United States and Canada is the most beautiful place in the world. I went there over the summer last year. But it's not the warmest place to go. The water is freezing, so I think I'll go to Mexico this year!

4 Linda

Last spring my family and I went to Vancouver and stayed at my aunt's house during spring break. It rained almost the entire time and the house was very cold, especially upstairs! But there are some cool places in Vancouver and some really great museums.

2 Read the sentences and say which person they refer to.

1 Who stayed in a place where the water is freezing?
2 Who went to Nevada?
3 Who saw strange rocks and trees?
4 Who stayed in a cold house?
5 Who will go to Mexico this year?
6 Who will go somewhere colder this year?

Listening

27 **3** **Listen and draw the correct weather symbols on the map.**

Key

☀	sunny
☁	rainy / showers
☁	cloudy
☁	snowy
≋	foggy
⚡☁	stormy/ thunderstorms
🚩	windy

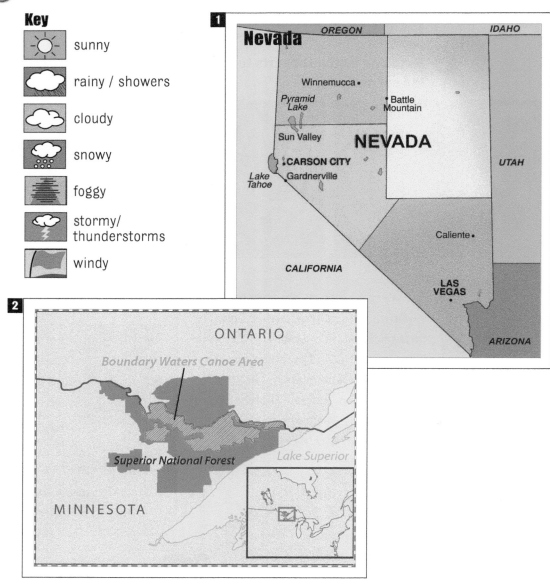

Speaking

4 **Work with a partner and discuss today's weather. What do you think it will be like tomorrow?**

A Today, the weather is…

B What will it be like tomorrow?

A I think it will be…

Speaking

5 Complete the quiz about your future. Then discuss your answers with a partner.

My Future!

When I am older, I think I will ...

	Yes	No		Yes	No
• go to college			• run a business		
• live in another country			• be rich		
• stay in the same place			• get married		
• live near my family			• drive a sports car		
• be an English teacher			• be famous		

A Will you go to college in the future?

B Yes, I will. / No, I won't. What about you?

Writing for your Portfolio

6 Read about Sarah's future and then write about yourself.

My future
I think I might be a famous explorer when I'm older because I like seeing different places and meeting people. I won't be very rich because I'll travel all the time. I'll live in the same country as I live now, near my family and friends, and I'll have a nice sports car and a beautiful house. What about you?

MORE fun with Fido

Aurora Borealis—the Northern Lights

Key words

cosmic weather	North / South Pole	moon	oxygen
high temperature	solar / lunar eclipse	phenomenon	nitrogen
particles	lightning	electric fields	oval-shaped
magnetic field	meteor	gas	

1 Read the texts.

The photos on this page show a "natural laser show" known as the Northern Lights. You can see this light show in many different countries in the world, including the northern United States and Canada. The Northern Lights are clearest during winter nights. During these nights, the sky often turns red, green, blue, or violet. Although we cannot always see them, the auroras are always there. They cover the North and South Pole and are oval-shaped.

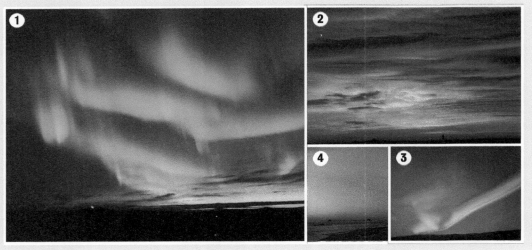

The Finnish name for the Northern Lights is *revontulet,* which means "fox fires." The name comes from an old story. It says that the arctic fox throws up snow with its big bushy tail. The snow goes high up into the sky and starts a fire, the "fox fire."

Some Inuit people, a native group in Alaska, were once scared of the Northern Lights. They thought they were very dangerous, especially for children. They told their children not to go outside when they were in the sky. They thought the Northern Lights would kill the children!

Where do the **Northern Lights** really come from?

2a **Read the text.**

What causes the different colors?

Auroras are always these pairs of colors–blue and red or green and brown–red. The colors of the aurora depend on which different gases are in the atmosphere. Nitrogen causes the blue and red lights and oxygen causes the green and brown–red lights. There is more nitrogen gas in the atmosphere nearest to Earth's surface. That is why the sky sometimes looks very red, almost like it's on fire.

2b **Look at the pictures of the Northern Lights on page 112. Decide if the main gas is nitrogen or oxygen.**

Mini-Project

3 **Complete the explanations for four other phenomena by using one of the words below to fill in the blank.**

rainbow	sun	lightning	moon

1 When there is a solar eclipse, the moon goes in front of the ……… .

2 When there is a lunar eclipse, Earth is between the ………… and the sun. Earth's shadow falls on the moon so we cannot see it.

3 A ……….. happens when it is raining and the light of the sun shines on the raindrops.

4 …………… happens when ice crystals and water drops in the air bump together to cause electricity.

4 **Choose one of the phenomena in Exercise 3. In small groups, draw a diagram to show how the phenomenon works. Use the Internet or a library to help you.**

UNIT (12) What if ...?

In this unit

You learn
- *If* clauses
- possessive pronouns
- questions with *Whose?*
- words for vacations

and then you can
- talk about alternatives
- talk about suggestions and preferences

1 Listen and read.

Mom Look. It says here if we book early, we'll get 10 percent off.

Sally What for?

Mom A vacation in a cabin on Lake Erie.

Harry I don't want to go there. There isn't enough to do. If you go there, I'll go and stay with Grandpa and Grandma.

Sally Well if he stays, I'll stay too. I'll go and stay with Lisa.

Dad No way! You're both coming with us.

Harry Staying with Lisa? Was that your idea or hers?

Sally Actually, it wasn't hers or mine. It was her parents' idea. They asked me last week.

Dad Well, I want us to take a vacation together as a family. What about taking a road trip to Aunt Maria's?

Sally Not again! It's way too far to drive.

Mom Well, why don't we go somewhere different, like Alaska? I've always wanted to go to Alaska.

Harry If we go there, I'll freeze. I can't stand cold weather.

Dad If we can't agree on something, we'll just have to stay home.

Harry Great! Then we can spend our summer vacation discussing next year's vacation!

2 **Complete the sentences.**

1 If they book early, they'll get…
2 Harry doesn't want to go to Lake Erie because…
3 Sally wants to stay…

4 Dad wants to go…
5 Mom has always wanted to…
6 Harry doesn't want to go to Alaska because…

Sounds right /iː/ /ɪ/

29 **3** **Listen. Circle the /iː/ sounds and underline the /ɪ/ sounds.**

freeze   is   we'll   swim   sea   if   beach   him   it

30 **4** **Now listen and repeat.**

We'll swim in the sea if it doesn't freeze.

Get talking Talking about alternatives

31 **5** **Listen and repeat.**

Girl Let's go to the beach.
Boy But what if it rains?
Girl Then we'll watch TV at your place.
Boy OK.

Boy Let's go swimming.
Girl But what if it's too cold?
Boy Then we won't stay in too long.

6 **Work with a partner. Match the phrases from columns A, B, and C to make dialogues similar to those in Exercise 5.**

	A		B		C
Let's…	• take the bus. • go to the movie theater. • use the computer. • go to Chile on vacation.	But what if…	• the bus is late. • the computer doesn't work. • it's too hot. • there are no more tickets.	Then	• we'll go and see another movie. • we'll write the letter. • we'll take sunscreen and hats. • we'll take a taxi.

Language Focus

Vocabulary Vacations

1 Write the correct numbers of the phrases in the pictures.

1 take a vacation	5 stay in a hotel	8 stay with relatives
2 go sightseeing	6 take photographs	9 go to the beach
3 buy souvenirs	7 go hiking	10 send postcards
4 go camping		

Get talking Suggestions and preferences

2 Listen and repeat.

A Let's go to Hawaii on vacation.
B Hawaii? No, I'd rather go to Mexico.

A Let's go camping this year.
B Camping? No, I'd rather go hiking.

3 Work with a partner. Make conversations like the ones in Exercise 2. Use the ideas in the boxes.

go to Seattle / go to New York City	stay in a hotel / stay with friends
stay in a hotel / go camping	go to the beach / go hiking
take photographs / write postcards	go sightseeing / buy souvenirs

Grammar

If clauses

1 **Put the words in order to make the examples. Check against the dialogue on page 114.**

we'll / we / book / If / get / early, / off. / 10 percent

go / If / there, / freeze. / we / I'll

To make a first conditional sentence, use the structure below:

If + subject + simple present / subject + **will/won't** + verb

If **you write** to her, **she'll be** very happy.

If **it's cold, we won't go** out.

If **you don't write** to her, **she'll be** unhappy.

If **it isn't** cold, **we'll go** out.

2 **Complete the sentences with the correct form of the verb.**

1 If we win the money, we .... (buy) a new house.

2 We .... (go) on vacation if there is time.

3 If we .... (need) some help, we'll ask.

4 She .... (not write) to you if she leaves.

5 If Harry stays with his grandparents, Sally .... (not be) happy.

6 We .... (do) this for you if you want.

3 **Circle the correct form to complete the sentences.**

1 If we *will win / win* the final, my team *will be / are* the best.

2 If you *do / don't do* what your teacher says, you *'ll be / be* in trouble.

3 If the phone *works / doesn't work*, we *return / 'll return* it to the store.

4 If you *will be / are* late, we *go / 'll go* to the movie theater without you.

5 If my parents *come back / will come back* from vacation, we *won't / will* have the party.

6 They *will buy / won't buy* the computer if it *will cost / costs* too much.

7 If he *is / will be* tired, he *will / won't* come.

4 **Complete the dialogue using the phrases below.**

> it rains   our parents say no
> 's no party

A Let's have an end-of-summer party on the beach on Friday.

B Good idea. But what if [1]........................ ?

C We can have the party at my place.

A Ok. But what if [2]........................ ?

D Then there [3]........................ !

5 Work with a partner. Student A chooses one of the suggestions below. Student B thinks of *But what if...* answers. Student A makes an alternative suggestion. Switch roles.

A We could take a bike ride next Sunday.
B Great idea. But what if it rains?
A We'll go the weekend after next!

Let's take a vacation to Arizona this year.

Let's write a school magazine in English and sell it to our parents.

Let's organize a football game against the teachers in our school.

We could go swimming on Saturday.

Possessive pronouns

6 **Look at the dialogue on page 114 and complete the examples.**

Was that your idea or ¹................?
Actually it wasn't ².............. or ³..............

my – **mine**	his – **his**	our – **ours**
your – **yours**	her – **hers**	your – **yours**
	its – **its**	their – **theirs**

We use possessive pronouns to say who something belongs to. We use them instead of a noun.
Was that your idea or **hers**? (= Was that your idea or **her idea**?)
It wasn't **hers** or **mine**. (= It wasn't **her idea** or **my idea**.)
I found this pen. Is it **yours**? (= Is it **your pen**?)
No, it's **his**. (= No, it's **his pen**.)

Questions with *Whose ...?*

Use *Whose...?* to ask who something belongs to.
"**Whose** coat is this?"   "It's Jane's." or "It's **hers**."

7 **Write questions with *Whose...?* and answers using possessive pronouns.**

1 this diary? – Tim's diary
   A *Whose diary is this*..............?
   B *It's his.*..............

2 these books? – Maria's books
   ....?
   ....

3 that camera? – my camera
   ....?
   ....

4 those black T-shirts – Mark and Harry's T-shirts
   ....?
   ....

5 these green sneakers – your sneakers
   ....?
   ....

Skills

Reading

1 How much do you remember about your English book? Take the quiz to find out.

✳ Book Quiz ✳

1 Abigail and Steve watched a scary DVD in Unit 2. What was its name?

- a ☐ *The Window*
- b ☐ *The Door*
- c ☐ *The Garden*

2 In Unit 3, Mark went on a trip and saw this. Where did he go?

- a ☐ Mexico
- b ☐ Indonesia
- c ☐ Guatemala

3 In Unit 4 you met this fantastic animal from Atlantis. What was it called?

- a ☐ a Snapkle
- b ☐ a Ruckle
- c ☐ a Hipcop

4 In Unit 5 Sally and Simon go on strike. Why? For:

- a ☐ more money
- b ☐ no more homework
- c ☐ no housework

5 This is Brittany from Unit 6. Which school did she go to?

- a ☐ Dance school
- b ☐ Drama school
- c ☐ Primary school

6 In Unit 7, Sally and Harry are going to visit this place. What is it called?

- a ☐ Six Flags
- b ☐ The Odeon
- c ☐ All Fun Park

7 What did Fido want in Unit 8?

- a ☐ chicken soup
- b ☐ a bone
- c ☐ steak and fries

8 In Unit 9 we met these people. What is the name of their planet?

- a ☐ Trojan
- b ☐ Juno
- c ☐ Jupiter

9 In Unit 10, Sally, Harry, and Olivia are trying to find a place. Which place?

- a ☐ the mall
- b ☐ the post office
- c ☐ the movie theater

10 In Unit 11, this student had a science test. What was his name?

- a ☐ Walter the Worrier
- b ☐ William the Worrier
- c ☐ William the Worker

Score ☐ / 10

Listening

  Listen and check your answers. Score 1 point for every answer you get right.

A Song 4 U We are on vacation

34 **3** **Listen and complete the song using the words on the left. Then sing along!**

classes
teachers
Maine
watch
rings
meet
plans
end
pack
beach

When the school bell ¹........................,
at a quarter to four,
and we ²........................ up our things,
and we walk out that door.
And we say goodbye,
to the ³........................ and friends,
it's the end of July
and school's at an ⁴........................ .

Chorus
We can do anything, we can go anywhere.
No more ⁵........................ for a long, long time.
We are on vacation, our summer vacation.
We're on vacation, we feel fine, we feel fine.

Do you have any ⁶........................
about what you do with your time?
Let's go to the ⁷........................
if the weather is fine.

Are you going away
to the Carolinas or ⁸........................ ?
Or are you going to stay
at home and play?

Chorus

If you feel bored,
just give me a call.
We can ⁹........................ up
at the mall.
Or see a movie
On DVD,
or instead we can
¹⁰........................ TV.

Chorus

Writing for your Portfolio

4 **Read Peter's plans for his next vacation. Then write about yourself.**

My next vacation
My next vacation is in July. I'm not sure what I'm going to do. We often go to Florida
and stay with my aunt and uncle. If my parents go there, I'll go with them. But
if we stay at home, I'll hang out with my friends and play video games and watch
DVDs and things like that.
I want to go to Florida because it's a lot of fun. The weather is always nice and
there are a lot of things to do.

MORE
fun
with
Fido

Check your progress Units 11 and 12

1 **Write the weather words.**

1 ....
2 ....
3 ....
4 ....
5 ....
6 ....
7 ....

☐ 7

2 **Complete with *will*, *won't*, or *might*.**

A I think it ¹.................. rain tomorrow.

B I don't think so. I think it ²..................
be sunny. It ³.................. be cloudy but it
definitely ⁴.................. be rainy.

A I think I ⁵.................. go to the beach.

B I ⁶.................. come with you or I
⁷.................. stay at home.

A ⁸.................. you come shopping with me now?

B OK! ☐ 8

3 **Complete the sentences with the correct possessive pronouns.**

1 This is Mark's book. It's ....
2 That was Mark and Sally's house. It was
....
3 This is my computer. It's ....
4 That was Sally's money. It was ....
5 This is your pen. It's ....

☐ 5

4 **Complete the first conditional sentences.**

1 If we stay at home, we .... (miss)
the show.
2 We .... (ask) about it, if you want.
3 If he .... (want) it, we'll buy it.
4 If it .... (not/work), we'll
return it.
5 They .... (not/go) on vacation
this year if their friends come to see them.

☐ 10

5 **Complete the dialogue. Use the first conditional.**

A ¹..................?
(you come to the concert / I buy the ticket)

B Yes, I ²..................

A I ³.................. (ask) Jack if he ⁴..................
(want) to come too. And Frankie.

B If Frankie ⁵.................. (come),
I ⁶.................. definitely go!

A OK. If I ⁷.................. (see) her, I ⁸..................
(ask) her.

B If she ⁹.................. (not want) to come,
I ¹⁰.................. (ask) her out somewhere
else.

A You must really like her! ☐ 10

6 **Write the questions.**

1 ....?
It's rainy and windy in Chicago.
2 ....?
No, they won't be here tomorrow.
3 ....?
Yes, he will pay for it.
4 ....?
No, it won't rain next week.
5 ....?
It's his car. ☐ 10

TOTAL ☐ 50

My progress so far is ...

☺ **great!** ☐
😐 **good.** ☐
☹ **poor.** ☐

UNIT 12 121

Extreme weather

1 Which photograph shows a hurricane and which a tornado?

HURRICANES
– THE FACTS –

* Hurricanes come from the ocean.
* They travel at more than 100 km per hour.
* They can be from 100 to 1,600 km wide.
* Hurricanes are given names, for example, Hurricane Andrew.

A

B

TORNADOES
– THE FACTS –

* There are about 800 to 1,200 tornadoes a year in the U.S.
* They are usually in Northwest Texas, Oklahoma, and Kansas.
* They circle around at speeds of 320 to 800 km per hour.
* They are a dark gray color because they pick up soil and other objects.

2 Read Jimmy's story and answer the questions.

1 When did Hurricane Katrina hit New Orleans?
2 Where was Jimmy when the hurricane happened?
3 How high did the water rise?
4 How fast was the wind?
5 How long did Jimmy wait to be rescued?

Jimmy's Story

In 2005, Hurricane Katrina hit New Orleans, and Jimmy Lewis's world fell apart. Jimmy stayed home, thinking that he would be able to make it through the hurricane. On Sunday night, the wind blew at 200km/hour. But Jimmy didn't worry—until water began to flood into his house. It filled up the first floor, then it filled up the second. Jimmy went into the attic. After a two-day wait, Jimmy was rescued. Now he feels lucky to be alive.

35

3 Listen and circle T (True) or F (False).

The Storm Chasers!
Most people run away or hide from hurricanes and tornadoes, but some people in the U.S. actually chase them! You can even take a storm-chasing vacation!

1 Storm-chasing tours are not safe. T / F
2 If you go on the tour, you will have breakfast at 8:00 a.m. T / F
3 The tornadoes are always far from the hotel. T / F
4 You can't take photos of the tornadoes. T / F
5 If there aren't any tornadoes, they go sightseeing. T / F

4 **Over 2 U!** Write about a weather disaster in your country.

MORE! Now you can watch Episode 6 of *Kids in NYC!* DVD

strange weather stories

Read MORE for pleasure

1 The day the sun rained

Once when I was a boy, I was playing football in the back yard of our house. It was a beautiful sunny day, but suddenly I saw some big black clouds in the sky. They were coming our way. I went to the front of the house to tell my mother, because the laundry was drying on the clothesline in the back yard. When I got to the front door, it was already raining heavily. My mother and I went to the back yard again, but when we got there, there was nothing but sun. It was very strange! When we looked one way, there was rain. When we looked the other way, there was sun. We call it "the day the sun rained."

2 Above the clouds

About five years ago, I was on vacation in New York City. It was really hot. The temperature was over 40°C. My friend and I decided to go to the top of the Empire State Building. "The air will be cooler up there," we thought. We were wrong, and it was very hot at the top, too. There were some clouds coming toward us and suddenly a thunderstorm started, but because we were so high up, the storm was below us. We looked down and saw the lightning and the rain falling, but we didn't get wet. It was so weird!

3 Raining frogs

I've got a really strange story about the weather. It's true, I promise, but not many people believe me. One day, when I was about 10, I was fishing with my brother when I saw a small frog hopping in the grass next to me. That wasn't strange. I was next to a river. But then I saw a splash in the water and another frog, and then another. I looked at my brother and he looked at me. We looked at the sky. There were some clouds but it wasn't raining. It was really strange. I looked at the ground. There were now about five frogs hopping about. Then I felt something hit me on my head. I put my hand on it and—yuck—there was a frog on top of me. It jumped off and then jumped away. After that we didn't see any more frogs or splashes. It sounds weird but I know that what we saw was frog rain.

For MORE! Go to www.cambridge.org/elt/americanmore and take a quiz on this text.

Wordlist

Unit 1

to bake /beɪk/
band /bænd/
bush /bʊʃ/
champion /'tʃæmpiən/
chess /tʃes/
choir /'kwaɪər/
colonization /ˌkɑːlənə'zeɪʃən/
cooking /'kʊkɪŋ/
dark /dɑːrk/
delicious /dɪ'lɪʃəs/
to discover /dɪs'kʌvər/
drama /'drɑːmə/
earthquake /'ɜːrθkweɪk/
explorer /ɪk'splɔːrər/
great /greɪt/
helicopter /'helikɑːptər/
hobby /'hɑːbi/
independent /ɪndɪ'pendənt/
island /'aɪlənd/
to join /dʒɔɪn/
to live /lɪv/
to miss /mɪs/
mission /'mɪʃən/
orchestra /'ɔːrkɪstrə/
peace /piːs/
population /ˌpɑːpjə'leɪʃən/
problem /'prɑːbləm/
republic /rɪ'pʌblɪk/
to rescue /'reskjuː/
technology /tek'nɑːlədʒi/
union /'juːnjən/
volleyball /'vɑːlibɔːl/

Unit 2

alone /ə'loʊn/
to answer /'ænsər/
awful /'ɑːfəl/
bank /bæŋk/
to believe /bɪ'liːv/
building /'bɪldɪŋ/
cartoon /kɑːr'tuːn/
cell /sel/
detective /dɪ'tektɪv/
to fall off /fɔːl 'ɑːf/
funny /'fʌni/

game show /'geɪm ʃoʊ/
to hang on /hæŋ 'ɑːn/
to hate /heɪt/
to hit /hɪt/
horror /'hɔːrər/
to invite /ɪn'vaɪt/
kids /kɪdz/
laptop /'læptɑːp/
to laugh /læf/
to leave /liːv/
to love /lʌv/
midnight /'mɪdnaɪt/
music video /'mjuːzɪk ˌvɪdioʊ/
nature program /'neɪtʃər ˌproʊgræm/
to need /niːd/
to order /'ɔːrdər/
quiz show /'kwɪz ʃoʊ/
to ring /rɪŋ/
sailing /'seɪlɪŋ/
scary /'skeri/
science fiction /ˌsaɪəns 'fɪkʃən/
shock /ʃɑːk/
sports show /'spɔːrts ʃoʊ/
strange /streɪndʒ/
the news /ðə 'nuːz/
to think /θɪŋk/
truck /trʌk/
to turn off /tɜːrn 'ɑːf/
voice /vɔɪs/
wave /weɪv/
weird /wɪrd/
western /'westərn/

Unit 3

basket /'bæskət/
bike /baɪk/
bus /bʌs/
to call /kɔːl/
car /kɑːr/
to change /tʃeɪndʒ/
to dig /dɪg/
to dream /driːm/
to drive /draɪv/
ferryboat /'feri ˌboʊt/

fool /fuːl/
gold /goʊld/
jaguar /'dʒægwɑːr/
jeep /dʒiːp/
jungle /'dʒʌŋgəl/
to lose /luːz/
metro /'metroʊ/
monkey /'mʌŋki/
moped /'moʊped/
museum /mjuː'ziːəm/
plane /pleɪn/
pyramid /'pɪrəmɪd/
school bus /ˌskuːl 'bʌs/
snake /sneɪk/
souvenir /suːvə'nɪr/
spider /'spaɪdər/
to stay /steɪ/
sunset /'sʌnset/
tent /tent/
ticket /'tɪkɪt/
tourist /'tʊrɪst/
tram /træm/
to visit /'vɪzɪt/
to wake up /weɪk 'ʌp/
wallet /'wɑːlɪt/

Unit 4

bad /bæd/
beautiful /'bjuːtəfəl/
big /bɪg/
bite /baɪt/
cheap /tʃiːp/
chimpanzee /ˌtʃɪmpæn'ziː/
coast /koʊst/
conversation /ˌkɑːnvər'seɪʃən/
curly /'kɜːrli/
cute /kjuːt/
dangerous /'deɪndʒərəs/
dragon /'drægən/
elephant /'eləfənt/
to exist /ɪg'zɪst/
exotic /ɪg'zɑːtɪk/
fairy tales /'feri ˌteɪlz/
to fish /fɪʃ/
glasses /'glæsɪz/

hip-hop /'hɪphɑːp/
mouse /maʊs/
owl /aʊl/
philosopher /fɪ'lɑːsəfər/
poisonous /'pɔɪzənəs/
to prefer /prɪ'fɜːr/
private /'praɪvət/
rabbit /'ræbɪt/
reptile /'reptaɪl/
researcher /'riːsɜːrtʃər/
sea level /'siː ˌlevəl/
short /ʃɔːrt/
slim /slɪm/
straight /streɪt/
strong /strɑːŋ/
sunken city /ˌsʌŋkən 'sɪti/
to talk /tɔːk/
tall /tɔːl/
ugly /'ʌgli/
underwater temples /ˌʌndərwɑːtər 'tempəlz/
wavy /'weɪvi/
wolf /wʊlf/
young /jʌŋ/

Unit 5

to argue /'ɑrgjuː/
to buy /baɪ/
canoeing trip /kə'nuːɪŋ ˌtrɪp/
to clean /kliːn/
to cook dinner /ˌkʊk 'dɪnər/
to do homework /ˌduː 'hoʊmwɜːrk/
to do the cleaning /ˌduː ðə 'kliːnɪŋ/
to do the dishes /ˌduː ðə 'dɪʃɪz/
to do the dusting /ˌduː ðə 'dʌstɪŋ/
fire /'faɪər/
to fly a plane /ˌflaɪ ə 'pleɪn/
football cleats /'fʊtbɔːl ˌkliːts/
to go grocery shopping /ˌgoʊ 'groʊsəri ˌʃɑːpɪŋ/
to go horseback riding /ˌgoʊ 'hɔːrsbæk ˌraɪdɪŋ/

to go on strike /ˌgoʊ ɑːn 'straɪk/

to have a party /ˌhæv ə 'pɑːrt̬i/

to help /help/

to iron the clothes /ˌaɪrn ðə 'kloʊðz/

to learn /lɜːrn/

to make the bed /ˌmeɪk ðə 'bed/

mess /mes/

messy /'mesi/

to move /muːv/

to play volleyball /ˌpleɪ 'vɑːlibɔːl/

to put something away /ˌpʊt ... ə'weɪ/

sister-in-law /'sɪstərɪnlɑː/

to stay at a friend's house /ˌsteɪ ət ə 'frendz ˌhaʊs/

to study /'stʌdi/

to take out the garbage /ˌteɪk aʊt ðə 'gɑːrbɪʤ

Unit 6

art /ɑːrt/

audition /ɑː'dɪʃən/

to borrow /'bɑːroʊ/

brain /breɪn/

to care /ker/

careful /'kerfəl/

circle /'sɜːrkəl/

computer science /kəm,pjuːtər 'saɪənts/

easy /'iːzi/

face /feɪs/

fair /fer/

fast /fæst/

figure /'fɪgjər/

file /faɪl/

to forget /fər'get/

geography /ʤi'ɑːgrəfi/

glad /glæd/

good /gʊd/

history /'hɪstəri/

to hurry /'hʌri/

math /mæθ/

to multiply /'mʌltɪplaɪ/

music /'mjuːzɪk/

physical education /ˌfɪzɪkəl ˌeʤʊ'keɪʃən/

polite /pə'laɪt/

to print out /prɪnt 'aʊt/

quick /kwɪk/

quiet /'kwaɪət/

racket /'rækɪt/

rectangle /'rektæŋgəl/

rule /ruːl/

schedule /'skeʤuːl/

science /'saɪənts/

slow /sloʊ/

square /skwer/

subject /'sʌbʤɪkt/

tonight /tə'naɪt/

triangle /'traɪæŋgəl/

to try /traɪ/

to turn off /tɜːrn 'ɑːf/

to understand /ˌʌndər'stænd/

workshop /'wɜːrkʃɑːp/

Unit 7

basketball /'bæskətbɔːl/

bike riding /'baɪk raɪdɪŋ/

to come back /kʌm 'bæk/

dinner /'dɪnər/

fan /fæn/

to get up late /ˌget ʌp 'leɪt/

to go fishing /goʊ 'fɪʃɪŋ/

to go shopping /goʊ 'ʃɑːpɪŋ/

to go to a friend's house /ˌgoʊ tuː ə 'frendz ˌhaʊs/

to go to the movies /ˌgoʊ tə ðə 'muːviz/

to hang out /hæŋ 'aʊt/

interested /'ɪntrɪstɪd/

to listen to music /ˌlɪsən tə 'mjuːzɪk/

mountain biking /'maʊntən ˌbaɪkɪŋ/

mountain climbing /'maʊntən ˌklaɪmɪŋ/

packed lunch /pækt 'lʌnʧ/

paper route /'peɪpər ˌraʊt/

plan /plæn/

to play sports /pleɪ 'spɔːrts/

to remember /rɪ'member/

running /'rʌnɪŋ/

to sell /sel/

skateboarding /'skeɪtbɔːrdɪŋ/

skating /'skeɪt̬ɪŋ/

surfing /'sɜːrfɪŋ/

swimming /'swɪmɪŋ/

theme park /'θiːm pɑːrk/

trampolining /ˌtræmpə'liːnɪŋ/

to watch sports /wɑːʧ 'spɔːrts/

Unit 8

anaconda /ˌænə'kɑːndə/

ankle /'æŋkəl/

antelope /'ænt̬ə,loʊp/

aspirin /'æsprɪn/

attack /ə'tæk/

backache /'bækeɪk/

blue whale /ˌbluː 'weɪl/

a cold /ə 'koʊld/

dentist /'dent̬ɪst/

dolphin /'dɑːlfɪn/

earache /'ɪreɪk/

environment /ɪn'vaɪrənmənt/

giraffe /ʤə'ræf/

a glass of water /ə ˌglæs əv 'wɑːt̬ər/

head /hed/

headache /'hedeɪk/

to hurt /hɜːrt/

knee /niː/

lemonade /ˌlemə'neɪd/

lion /'laɪən/

lucky /'lʌki/

medicinal /mə'dɪsɪnəl/

ostrich /'ɑːstrɪʧ/

oxygen /'ɑːksɪʤən/

painting /'peɪnt̬ɪŋ/

pig /pɪg/

plant /plænt/

project /'prɑːʤekt/

rain forest /'reɪn ˌfɔːrɪst/

rhinoceros /raɪ'nɑːsərəs/

romantic /roʊ'mænt̬ɪk/

safe /seɪf/

sick /sɪk/

sore throat /sɔːr 'θroʊt/

stomach /'stʌmək/

stomachache /'stʌmək ˌeɪk/

streetlight /'striːt laɪt/

toe /toʊ/

toothache /'tuːθeɪk/

to wake /weɪk/

whale shark /'weɪl ʃɑːrk/

Unit 9

air /er/

aliens /'eɪliənz/

around /ə'raʊnd/

to block /blɑːk/

bored /bɔːrd/

button /'bʌtən/

to carry /'kæri/

coffee /'kɑːfi/

comfortable /'kʌmfərt̬əbəl/

country /'kʌntri/

to cry /kraɪ/

to destroy /dɪ'strɔɪ/

dirty /'dɜːrt̬i/

frightened /'fraɪtənd/

garbage can /'gɑːrbɪʤ ˌkæn/

gas company /'gæs ˌkʌmpəni/

gas leak /'gæs ˌliːk/

to go out /goʊ 'aʊt/

huge /hjuːʤ/

key /kiː/

to land /lænd/

lights /laɪts/

to lock /lɑːk/

loud /laʊd/

mask /mæsk/

palace /'pæləs/

path /pæθ/

to pick up /pɪk 'ʌp/

place /pleɪs/

planet /'plænɪt/

to push /pʊʃ/

to run away /rʌn ə'weɪ/

salt /sɔːlt/

seed /siːd/

shocked /ʃɑːkt/

silver /'sɪlvər/

spaceship /'speɪʃɪp/
to steal /stiːl/
still /stɪl/
suddenly /'sʌdənli/
surprised /sər'praɪzd/
thrilled /θrɪld/
to turn around /tɜːrn ə'raʊnd/
universe /'juːnəvɜːrs/
world /wɜːrld/

Unit 10

to be lost /ˌbiː 'lɔːst/
to cross /krɑːs/
crowd /kraʊd/
directions /də'rekʃənz
to explain /ɪk'spleɪn/
to fall asleep /fɔːl ə'sliːp/
to figure something out /ˌfɪgjər...'aʊt/
gas station /'gæs ˌsteɪʃən/
to go around in circles /ˌgoʊ əˌraʊnd ɪn 'sɜːrkəlz/
go as far as the... /'goʊ əz ˌfɑːr əz ðə/
go past the... /'goʊ pæst ðə/
go straight ahead /ˌgoʊ streɪt ə'hed/
hospital /'hɑːspɪtəl/
hotel /hoʊ'tel/
map /mæp/
now /naʊ/
one hundred /ˌwʌn 'hʌndrəd/
one hundred thousand /wʌn ˌhʌndrəd 'θaʊzənd/
one million /ˌwʌn 'mɪljən/
one thousand /ˌwʌn 'θaʊzənd/
police station /pə'liːs ˌsteɪʃən/
post office /'poʊst ˌɑːfɪs/
to rent a DVD /ˌrent ə ˌdiː viː 'diː/
restaurant /'restərɑːnt/
star /stɑːr/
take the first left /ˌteɪk ðə ˌfɜːrst 'left/
take the second right /ˌteɪk ðə ˌsekənd 'raɪt/

tourist office /'tʊrɪst ˌɑːfɪs/
traffic /'træfɪk/
turn left /ˌtɜːrn 'left/
turn right /ˌtɜːrn 'raɪt/
way /weɪ/
welcome /'welkəm/

Unit 11

beach /biːtʃ/
blanket /'blæŋkɪt/
breeze /briːz/
championship /'tʃæmpiənʃɪp/
clouds /klaʊdz/
cloudy /'klaʊdi/
college /kɑːlɪdʒ/
to come out /kʌm 'aʊt/
degree /dɪ'griː/
explorer /ɪk'splɔːrər/
famous /'feɪməs/
fog /fɑːg/
foggy /'fɑːgi/
to get married /ˌget 'merid/
no way /noʊ 'weɪ/
outside /aʊt'saɪd/
to pass /pæs/
race /reɪs/
rain /reɪn/
rainy /'reɪni/
rich /rɪtʃ/
showers /'ʃaʊərz/
sky /skaɪ/
snow /snoʊ/
snowy /'snoʊi/
sun /sʌn/
sunny /'sʌni/
thunderstorm /'θʌndərstɔːrm/
upstairs /ʌp'sterz/
windy /'wɪndi/

Unit 12

to agree /ə'griː/
bell /bel/
to book /bʊk/
discount /'dɪskaʊnt/
to discuss /dɪ'skʌs/
down /daʊn/
to freeze /friːz/

to go on vacation /ˌgoʊ ɑːn veɪ'keɪʃən/
to go sightseeing /ˌgoʊ 'saɪtsiːɪŋ/
idea /aɪ'diə/
magazine /'mægəˌziːn/
to organize /'ɔːrgənaɪz/
postcard /'poʊstkɑːrd/
relatives /'relətɪvz/
sunscreen /'sʌnskriːn/
trouble /'trʌbəl/
weather /'weðər/
would rather /wʊd 'ræðər/

Pronunciation guide

Vowels

/iː/	**re**a**l**, scr**ee**n
/ɪ/	d**i**sh, s**i**t
/i/	funn**y**
/e/	ch**e**ss, b**e**d
/æ/	b**a**d, t**a**xi
/ʌ/	m**u**st, d**o**ne
/ʊ/	g**oo**d, f**u**ll
/uː/	ch**oo**se, vi**ew**
/ə/	dr**a**matic, th**e**
/ɑː/	st**o**p, **o**pera
/ɔː/	s**aw**, d**au**ghter

Vowels + /r/

/ɜːr/	f**ir**st, sh**ir**t
/ɑːr/	c**ar**
/ɔːr/	h**or**se
/er/	th**eir**
/ʊr/	t**our**ist
/ɪr/	**ear**
/ər/	teach**er**

Diphthongs

/eɪ/	pl**ay**, tr**ai**n
/aɪ/	**i**ce, n**igh**t
/ɔɪ/	empl**oy**er, n**oi**sy
/aʊ/	h**ou**se, d**ow**nload
/oʊ/	n**o**, wind**ow**

Consonants

/p/	**p**ush
/b/	**b**ank
/t/	**t**ime
/t̮/	bu**tt**er
/d/	**d**iary
/k/	**c**arpet
/g/	bi**g**
/f/	sur**f**
/v/	**v**ery
/θ/	**th**in
/ð/	**th**at
/s/	**s**it
/z/	**z**ero
/ʃ/	**sh**ine
/ʒ/	mea**s**ure
/h/	**h**ot
/w/	**w**ater
/tʃ/	**ch**air
/dʒ/	**j**oke
/m/	**m**ore
/n/	s**n**ow
/ŋ/	si**ng**
/r/	**r**ing
/l/	sma**ll**
/j/	**y**ou

CAMBRIDGE UNIVERSITY PRESS
www.cambridge.org/elt/americanmore

HELBLING LANGUAGES
www.helblinglanguages.com

American MORE! 2 Student's Book
by Herbert Puchta & Jeff Stranks
with G. Gerngross C. Holzmann P. Lewis-Jones

© Cambridge University Press and Helbling Languages 2010
(More was originally published by Helbling Languages © Helbling Languages 2006)

6th printing 2016

Printed in Italy by Rotolito Lombarda S.p.A.

ISBN 978-0-521-17126-7   American MORE! 2 Student's Book with interactive CD-ROM
ISBN 978-0-521-17131-1   American MORE! 2 Workbook with Audio CD
ISBN 978-0-521-17128-1   American MORE! 2 Teacher's Book
ISBN 978-0-521-17127-4   American MORE! Teacher's Resource Pack with Testbuilder CD-ROM / Audio CD
ISBN 978-0-521-17133-5   American MORE! 2 Class Audio CDs
ISBN 978-0-521-17134-2   American MORE! 2 Extra Practice Book
ISBN 978-0-521-17135-9   American MORE! 2 DVD (NTSC)

The authors would like to thank those people who have made significant contributions towards the final form of MORE! INTERNATIONAL:

Oonagh Wade and Rosamund Cantalamessa for their expertise in working on the manuscripts, their useful suggestions for improvement, and the support we got from them.

Lucia Astuti and Markus Spielmann, Helbling Languages, Ron Ragsdale and James Dingle, Cambridge University Press, for their dedication to the project and innovative publishing vision.

Our designers, Amanda Hockin, Greg Sweetnam, Quantico, Craig Cornell and Niels Gyde for their imaginative layouts and stimulating creativity. Also, our artwork assistants, Silvia Scorzoso and Francesca Gironi, for their dedicated work.

The publishers would like to thank the following for their kind permission to reproduce the following photographs and other copyright material:

The publishers would like to thank the following for their kind permission to reproduce the following photographs and other copyright material:
Alamy p5 (CD: Ultimate Food; Shakira; Tom Cruise; group playing music), p6, p10 (teenager making model), p12 (settlers), p22, p26, p28, p30, p31, p35 (CD: Ultimate Food; hip hop singer), p39, p41, p42, p50, p51, p52 (Robo Cup; Autonomous Underwater Vehicle; Car Factory), p59, p60, p62, p64 (Alton Towers), p66, p68, p69, p71, p72 (cave drawings), p75 (girl listening to music; girl watching TV; boy running), p78, p79, p80, p81, p82, p85, p92, p93, p102, p109, p111, p119, p122; **Can Stock Photo** p109 (Juan); **Corbis** p79 (elephant),
p102 (policemen on bikes), p109 (Mel), p122 (storm chaser); **Günter Gerngross** (small plane; jeep) p30; **Helbling Languages** p53 (DVD player; bicycle; mp3); ©**iStockphoto.com** p5 (lasagne), p6 (school orchestra; class watching video), p9, p10, p12 (traffic), p26 (bus), p35, p41 (bus), p43, p52 (robots), p53, p56, p66 (man surfing), p72, p73 p75, p81 (man surfing), p83, p102 (Mustang; Model T Ford), p109 (canoe, Joshua Tree), p110, p112, p116 p122 (damage left by hurricane Katrina); **Library of Congress** p12 (San Francisco); © **Little, Brown** p93 (Maniac Magee); **Photos.com** p23, p26 (school bus; ferryboat, metro), p41 (school bus; ferryboat); **Shutterstock** p6 (football players), p12 (mission at San Diego), p24, p26 (taxi), p57 (stop sign; no parking sign; no bicycles sign), p102 (Cadillac), p109 (Vancouver; Linda); **SuperStock** p6 (marching band), p12 (man panning for gold); **The Random House Group Ltd.** p93 (VickyAngel); **The Times Herald of Norristown, Penn** p92 (Jerry Spinelli); © **XiLanWu - Fotolia.com** p29.

The publishers would like to thank the following illustrators:

Roberto Battestini; Lucy Boden; Dan Chernett; Moreno Chiacchiera; Kelly Dyson; Michele Farella; Giovanni Giorgi Pierfranceschi; Pierluigi Longo; Gastone Mencherini; David Shephard.

The publishers would like to thank the following for their assistance with commissioned photographs:

Ed-Imaging pp 4, 14, 24, 34, 44, 54, 64, 74, 84, 94, 104, 114; **David Tolley Ltd.** p76.

Every effort has been made to trace the owners of any copyright material in this book. If notified, the publisher will be pleased to rectify any errors or omissions.